REGNUM STUDIES

Mission Possible

The Biblical Strategy for Reaching the Lost

REGNUM STUDIES IN MISSION

A full listing of all titles in this series
appears at the close of this book

Mission Possible

The Biblical Strategy for Reaching the Lost

Julie C. Ma

Foreword by Walter C. Kaiser, Jr

regnum

First published 2005 by Paternoster

Paternoster is an imprint of Authentic Media
9 Holdom Avenue, Bletchley, Milton Keynes, MK1 1QR, UK
and
PO Box 1047, Waynesboro, GA 30830–2047, USA

11 10 09 08 07 06 05   7 6 5 4 3 2 1

British Library Cataloguing in Publication Data
A catalogue record for this book is available from the British Library

ISBN 1-870345-37-1

Typeset by A.R. Cross
Printed and bound in the Philippines
for Paternoster
by SCR Printing

To
Wonsuk,
my treasured partner in life and ministry

Contents

Chapter 3

Chapter 4

Excursus 2

Chapter 5

Foreword

Mission Possible: The Biblical Strategy for Reaching the Lost is right on target. And it is indeed a 'Mission Possible!' Ever since the promise was given to Eve, Shem and Abraham early in Genesis, it has been the plan of God to bring the gospel to every tribe, tongue and nation on planet earth. No wonder the Apostle Paul carefully labeled the essence of the promise-plan of God given in its rudimentary form in Genesis 12:3 ('In your Seed shall all the nations of the earth be blessed') as nothing less than the 'gospel' itself. There Paul proclaimed: 'The Scripture foresaw that God would justify the Gentiles by faith, announced the gospel in advance to Abraham: "All nations will be blessed through you"' (Galatians 3:8, NIV).

The mission of God cannot be described more succinctly nor more accurately: It remains God's distinctive work through the powerful agency of the Holy Spirit. But it refuses to be cornered or be captured by any one nationality, social class, gender, or the like. It is for all men and women, boys and girls, who are made in God's image and for whom the Messiah, Christ Jesus, lived, died and rose again in his work on the cross that provided atonement for all, past, present and future who will repent and believe in him.

But lest anyone think that this plan has slowed down recently or is in trouble, let it be boldly announced that the gospel of Jesus Christ and his wonderful and loving gift of redemption is having enormous success, especially in the two-thirds world. In almost every spot on the globe, except in western Europe, Canada, and the United States (with some outstanding exceptions), the power of Christ's word to save is being received in unprecedented numbers. The last two or three decades have seen one of the greatest unreported news stories of either the twentieth or twenty-first century. This is currently being documented by the Study for Global Christianity and can be accessed from the Gordon-Conwell Theological Seminary web site. In fact, the geographical center of the population trusting in Christ as their personal Savior moved from Jerusalem in the first Christian century on to the middle of Europe during the reformation, but is now found in the middle of Africa.

Do more than enjoy Julie's beautifully written strategy. May it prompt a whole new involvement of the whole body of Christ to a renewed sense of prayer, service and study of God's Word. All too frequently the biblical basis for carrying out this strategy is referred to somewhat summarily. But Scripture is the key to our understanding and the ministry of the Holy Spirit's powerful use of that Word of God. May your reading of this book convince you that the whole Bible is filled with this call for action as one of its central themes. What could be a greater challenge for mission or for obedient response to our Lord than to patiently hear what he wants to say to us his Church through his Word as the first line of action. May our Lord send us 'times of refreshing from above' as believers are revived and many are daily being added to the family of God.

Walter C. Kaiser, Jr.
President
Colman M. Mockler Distinguished Professor of Old Testament
Gordon-Conwell Theological Seminary
Hamilton, MA, USA

Preface

For a long time I have wanted to write a mission book 'written by foot,' that is, written as I hike the mountains to share God's good news; a missiology book 'for the rest of us,' so that missiology will become liberated from the specialists to every believer. Also, in my annual teaching of Biblical Foundation of Mission in Asia, the need for a textbook that is simple and friendly, and yet solid in biblical interpretation became apparent. Linking the biblical teaching to the actual and contemporary mission account serves several important purposes. First, Asian minds in many non-western worlds learn more effectively as examples are given. Second, the biblical development is brought to our contemporary setting, making the Bible ours for the twenty-first century.

This book, like many others, owes a great debt to the countless missionary minds that diligently studied the Scriptures. My students coming from many Asian countries have contributed greatly. Many of them had to undergo unbelievable persecution, often risking their very lives for the cause of their faith. Their reflection on the Scriptures is not for academic interest but for an existential purpose. These testimonies make the Scriptures truly alive. However, how this Asian context can influence the interpretation of the Bible is a continuing quest.

This book is also a cooperative project. Wonsuk, my husband, has been a constant encouragement, as my two boys, Woolim and Boram, have prayed for this book. It also serves as a special celebration volume for Woolim's commitment to missionary work. Drs Vinay Samuel and Chris Sugden of Regnum Books International graciously approved the publication of this book through its prestigious publishing house. Mr Jeremy Mudditt and his able staff at Paternoster assisted me in the publication process. The careful editorial help of Dr Anthony R. Cross of Paternoster drastically improved the book. Daniel Kim, my student, rendered valuable assistance for the index, while Kathy Baxter, a missionary to the Philippines, proofread the entire book. The Faculty Publication Assistance program of Asia Pacific Theological Seminary provided valuable financial assistance. This fund was provided by the Boys and Girls Missionary Crusade (BGMC) administered by the Northern Asia Regional Office (Rev. Ron Maddux, director), Assemblies of God World Mission, Springfield, MO, USA.

May the Lord use this book to impress more minds that God's mission is absolutely possible.

Julie C. Ma
April 2004
Baguio, Philippines

Introduction

This book aims to discuss significant biblical themes which contain important missiological implications. Although Bible believers have some understanding that God initiated, planned and will accomplish his mission, many may not have a concrete picture as to how his mission plan developed throughout the Scriptures. Thus, it is necessary to trace the development of the mission themes in the Bible in order to understand his mission purpose and his call upon Israel and the church to fulfill his saving work. Each chapter investigates one of these themes.

Chapter 1 discusses God's salvation plan revealed in history: it starts from the fall of Adam and Eve. Then it moves to Noah where we can discover God's providence for the whole creation through the covenant of the rainbow which signifies God's promise not to destroy, but to protect and provide for them. The Abrahamic covenant reveals an important plan of God's mission: to begin a new race that will fulfill God's plan. God also promised Abraham to be a spiritual and physical blessing to his own people and the nations who will later join his heirs. Moses was called to be a part of God's mission purpose. He gave Moses and Israel the law for them to live holy lives as his chosen people. God's intention of the election of Israel is clear. The Davidic covenant is intended to introduce the 'Seed' of David through which all humanity will be saved. His shed blood on the cross is the ultimate climax of God's plan of redemption.

Charter 2 delineates the concept of light through the Old and New Testaments. God's purpose of calling Israel is for them to be light to the nations through holy living. The book of Isaiah is particularly important in contributing to the development of this theme. In Acts, Paul and Barnabas referred to this concept as the theological foundation for their missionary work.

Chapter 3 traces the expansion of God's divine work to the nations. This discussion notes that God is not only the God of Israel but of the nations, in spite of their ignorance of God's existence and work among and for humanity and his creation. The chapter further argues that God is absolutely unlimited as he freely uses non-Israelites in accomplishing his intention.

Chapter 4 describes God's power in mission. He revealed his power in different ways. The Israelites experienced his greatness through manifestation of his power. Such concrete experience enabled them to understand God in a convincing way. Jesus' earthly ministry is also marked by it: often miracles provided an eye-opening experience for people to follow him. Unfortunately, this important aspect of God's plan is often ignored in missions.

Chapter 5 focuses on the ministry of Jesus which was consistently marked by the presence of the Spirit. His mission was well defined: proclaiming good news by liberating and freeing those who are held captives in bondage, delivering those who are crying out to him. Also, his preparation for mission is discussed as he spent time in the desert for forty days of prayer and fasting. This provided him with spiritual strength and power for the perfect accomplishment of God's mission.

Chapter 6 discusses the Great Commission as God's mandate for his church. Cast in a post-resurrection scene, various terms contained in this command are studied. Also the universal nature of the mandate is noted, along with the promise of Jesus to them: 'I will be with you,' which serves as the supreme guarantee of God's presence.

Chapter 7 describes the expansion of the church through the book of Acts. This begins with the Lord's command to his disciples to be witnesses starting in Jerusalem, Judea, Samaria, and going to the ends of the earth. The Holy Spirit empowered them, and the book of Acts provides concrete cases of the expansion of the church by the Holy Spirit. Persecution became a factor to speed this process by scattering believers to many corners of the world to fulfill God's plan. This chapter shows how the good news and its carrier, the church, spread through the sacrificial work of the disciples.

The last chapter discusses incarnational mission: understanding the minds of people, identifying with them in sorrow and joy. The internal and external attitude of the followers of Christ is critical in the presentation of the gospel to people. Although the message is essential, the life of a gospel bearer is also part of the message itself. Thus, the godly lifestyle of the witnesses becomes part of God's mandate for mission. This is where the diligent study of cultures and worldview become important.

This study of God's revelation through mission is augmented by several stories of mission that came from my own missionary work. They are not just to illustrate the biblical points, but serve as the extension of God's missionary work recorded in the Bible. They also demonstrate how the gospel is received and perceived in a different context. The gospel will play its role when it is well planted in the hearts of people through the endeavor and effort of our mission.

CHAPTER 1

The History of God's Salvation

I. Introduction

The platform of God's revelation is human history. Likewise, the unfolding of God's plan for human salvation is also through human history, making history 'his story.' As much as history is a record of human failure, it also reveals God's brilliant work to save humanity. At the center of this great plan of human salvation are carefully selected human agents through whom God either reveals his specific plan or through whom he begins a long and complex line from which the Savior would come. These individuals functioned like stepping stones across the river of salvation.

This study is intended to trace the trajectory of 'God's story' in human history. More specifically I plan to look at important human agents of God's salvation, the stepping stones through whom God's plan of salvation has been thus far fulfilled. The study naturally begins with Adam, and progresses through various 'covenants' until the plan realizes its grand fulfilment in the life of Jesus.

II. Agents of God's Salvation

2.1 Adam

Genesis 3 recounts the fall of humankind and God's subsequent punishment of them. The serpent tempted the woman with the question, 'Did God really say, "You must not eat from any tree in the garden?"' The snake's very approach illustrates its shrewdness as the woman was targeted. Perhaps he chose Eve because a woman is not naturally as strong as a man, or because she had not received God's command directly from him, but through Adam (2:16). The tempter's skillful approach was manifested by his clever step-by-step enticement.[1]

There are different interpretations about the identity of the serpent. Nonetheless, it is generally recognized to be Satan in disguise. As

---

[1] H.C. Leupold, *Exposition of Genesis* (Grand Rapids, MI: Baker, 1984), I,.143.

commonly understood, Satan is the real tempter and holds the 'power of temptation'.[2] This has been an old and long-standing Christian exegesis. Two other interpretations are: 1) 'the serpent is purely symbolical; it symbolizes human curiosity' or 'intellectual curiosity', and 2) the serpent is an animal that is exceptionally smart as verse 1 says.[3]

Verses 4-5 detail the process of the temptation. The serpent contradicted the word God spoke to Adam and Eve. In verse 3 God said, 'You must not eat fruit from the tree that is in the middle of the garden, and you must not touch it, or you will die.' However, the serpent lied to her saying 'You will not surely die,' but 'you will be like God, knowing good and evil' (vv. 4-5).

Claus Westermann points out,

> The expression 'to know good and evil', is to be understood as a whole... This way of knowing is not a knowledge of some thing, of an object, as it is very often explained; it is rather a functional knowledge. 'Good and evil' does not mean something that is good or evil in itself, but what is good or evil for human beings, i.e., what is useful or harmful. Knowledge that is related to what is useful or injurious is to be thought of in the context of the struggle for existence. The person, by knowing and distinguishing the useful and the injurious, masters one's obligations and brings them to fruition. This is just what the woman says as she reflects in v. 6: '...to be desired to make one wise'; the verb here can also translated 'succeed.' Success is made possible by distinguishing between good and evil.[4]

Thus, knowledge here is a broader and more comprehensive concept.[5] As mentioned above, 'to know good and evil' is largely to be viewed as a practical knowledge.

This desire caused her to covet the forbidden fruit. The man associates with the woman in the eating (cf. 6:18; 7:7; 13:1). Indeed, that was the final and decisive act of disobedience, immediately the result of their sin is described. This strong human desire to obtain the knowledge of good and evil brought about the downfall of, not only the first couple, but also of all humanity. Verse 9 states that God sought man. According to Cassuto, 'the Lord God called' suggests the Judge of the entire world was calling man to charge him to give an account of his behavior.[6] The couple emerged shamefully from the trees (v. 10). It is assumed from

---

[2] Claus Westermann, *Genesis: A Practical Commentary*, trans. David E. Green (Grand Rapids, MI: Eerdmans, 1985), 22.

[3] Claus Westermann, *Genesis 1-11: A Commentary*, trans. John J. Scullion (Minneapolis, MN: Augsburg, 1984), 237.

[4] Westermann, *Genesis 1-11*, 241.

[5] J. Wellhausen, *Die Composition des Hexateuchs und der historischen Bücher des Alten Testaments* (Berlin: W. de Gruyter, 1963), 301.

[6] U. Cassuto, *A Commentary on the Book of Genesis 1-11*, trans. I. Abrahams (Jerusalem: Magnes, 1964), 155.

their response to God's call that they understood that the question, 'Where are you?' was a request to explain their action (vv. 11-13).

In Genesis 3:14-16 God cursed both the serpent and the woman:

> 'Cursed are you above all the livestock and all the wild animals! You will crawl on your belly and you will eat dust all the days of your life. And I will put enmity between you and the woman, and between your offspring and hers; he will crush your head and you will strike his heel.' To the woman he said, 'I will greatly increase your pains in childbearing; with pain you will give birth to children: Your desire will be for your husband, and he will rule over you.'

Here, eating dust does not mean to live in the dirt, rather it is figurative for humiliation, particularly by enemies (cf. Ps. 72:9; Isa. 49:23; Mic. 7:17). The serpent was to be humiliated throughout his life.[7] The serpent is more cursed than all the other animals (v. 14). Traditionally, verse 15 is interpreted not only literally or figuratively but also spiritually.

From the period of Irenaeus, Christian tradition has viewed the passage (v. 15) as a foretelling of Christ. Thus, the 'seed of the woman' has been interpreted as being a distinctive descendant who would crush the head of the serpent, that is, Satan. A fierce battle would ensue with the 'seed of the woman', and Satan would at last succumb to the seed of the woman. This viewpoint from Irenaeus allows an exegetical opportunity in both the Catholic and the Evangelical traditions.[8] 'In the course of the Middle Ages, Irenaeus' interpretation of the *Protoevangelium* found a firm place in theology. It won its final victory at the beginning of the modern era when it was acknowledged in dogmatic encyclicals of the highest church authority.'[9]

The messianic interpretation of verse 15 is also found in late Judaism.[10] The serpent is seen as the idealization of a demonic power, stressing the enmity between the human race and the evil power.[11] The passage is an assurance of victory over the devil to humankind, by being joined to Christ its divine Head.[12] Although some theologians have questioned this interpretation, in Protestant theology it is commonly accepted.

Verse 16 contains God's curse on women during pregnancy. She will suffer pain in childbearing and pangs in childbirth. The woman will suffer from pregnancy throughout her life. The man's sentence follows in verses 17-19. He will have unremitting toil all the days of his life.

---

[7] Westermann, *Genesis 1-11*, 79.

[8] Westermann, *Genesis 1-11*, 260.

[9] Westermann, *Genesis 1-11*, 261.

[10] John Skinner, *Genesis: Critical and Exegetical Commentary* (Edinburgh: T. & T. Clark, 1969), 81. Also see Robert Alter, *Genesis: Translation and Commentary* (London and New York: W.W. Norton, 1996), 13.

[11] Westermann, *Genesis 1-11*, 261.

[12] Skinner, *Genesis*, 81.

For Adam and Eve the primary and real curse is banishment from the garden and alienation from God. The couple is expelled for their disobedience to God. Removal from the garden and consequently the loss of nearness to God expresses humanity's present condition of existence with its limitations.[13]

In conclusion, by listening to Satan's temptation to doubt God's goodness, the woman deviates from the divine rule set by God and sin entered the world. However, a word of hope and assurance is given and curses and punishments are also given. The covenant of God given to Adam and Eve is a divine guarantee that through the 'seed of a woman', Jesus Christ, they will triumph over Satan. Christ will defeat this enemy (Satan) and bring an ultimate victory.

2.2 Noah

Although the history of mission starts with Abraham, the covenant with Noah in Genesis 9:8-17 precedes the covenant with Abraham. Some missiologists have declared that Noah's covenant is the real groundwork for God's mission for humanity. The covenant with Noah, sealed with the sign of God's 'bow in the cloud', is significant in declaring the universal purpose of salvation revealed in the Old Testament.[14] Noah's covenant is intended for all humanity: 'My covenant [is] between me and you and all living creatures of every kind.' This covenant is a promise and assurance that God will protect and preserve all humankind. Whereas, the covenant with Abraham is a promise to a particular individual, its purpose is to fulfill the universal mission of God.

There are far-reaching commonalities and an interrelationship between the flood account and the creation story. For example, there was a moment of chaos in the account of man's creation in Genesis 2:18. The flood narrative likewise starts negatively saying that those whom God made have failed: people are evil (6:5-6) and the earth is corrupt (6:11-12). 'Both [narratives] begin with a decision of God about humanity; both envisage the possibility of the failure of humanity as God's creation; both are concerned with the existence or non-existence of humanity.'[15] Thus, these two events are apparently interconnected.

The flood story depicts God in a completely different way than the typical ancient theological understanding: portraying him as the only existing God. This implies that all power belongs to him: it is not shared among different gods. He is revealed to be personal as anthropomorphic

---

[13] Westermann, *Genesis 1-11*, 257.

[14] Bengt Sundker, *The World of Mission* (Grand Rapids, MI: Eerdmans, 1965), 11.

[15] Westermann, *Genesis 1-11*, 393.

language is freely employed to depict God's thoughts and attitudes.[16] Verse 6, for example, says, 'The Lord was grieved that he had made man on the earth, and his heart was filled with pain.' God has an emotional dimension as though he were human. Humanity's wickedness causes grief to God. Every preference of the thoughts of their heart was only evil (v. 5). His grief led to divine punishment (v. 7).

In the midst of God's judgment, however, he planned to save humanity by preserving a man, Noah, who became a hope of restoration for God's creation.

Noah is described as righteous, blameless and perfect among his generation. Here, the word 'righteous' is synonymous with 'innocent' and 'upright.' He was a good man who followed God's principles of behavior. Noah walked with God like Enoch (5:22, 24), the only other person named to have done so.[17] Noah was not only a man of righteousness but also a man of obedience and faith. He believed the divine words of warning (chs. 6 and 7).

Genesis 7:4 records that rain came on the earth for forty days and forty nights. Verse 24 reports, 'The waters flooded the earth for a hundred and fifty days', presumably from the beginning of the rain (7:11) to the resting of the ark on the ground (8:4). The water was everywhere, as if the whole world had turned to its original chaotic state. Nothing is left of the abundant life that was brought forth upon the earth.[18] Total destruction of the earth was the divine punishment.

However, following the flood on the earth, God positions himself differently and forges an everlasting covenant with Noah. Genesis 9:12-16 clearly speaks of God's promise to Noah and humankind.

> This is the sign of the covenant I am making between me and you and every living creature with you, a covenant for all generations to come. I have set my rainbow in the clouds, and it will be the sign of the covenant between me and the earth. Whenever I bring clouds over the earth and the rainbow appears in the clouds, I will remember my covenant between me and you and all living creatures of every kind. Never again will the waters become a flood to destroy all life. Whenever the rainbow appears in the clouds, I will see it and remember the everlasting covenant between God and all living creatures of every kind on the earth.

The rainbow (v. 13) reminds God of his own covenant not to destroy the human race again. This is a one-sided promise: all flesh will never again be cut off by a flood (v. 11). The sign is often connected with the covenant (Gen. 21:30; 38:17) as 'a pledge of the assurance'

---

[16] Gordon J. Wenham, *Genesis 1-15*, Word Biblical Commentary 1 (Waco, TX: Word Books, 1987), 165.

[17] Wenham, *Genesis 1-15*, 169-70.

[18] Cassuto, *A Commentary on the Book of Genesis 1-11*, 97.

underscoring that it is God alone who is speaking in the 'covenant.' Further, it is God who places himself under responsibility ('self-obligation').[19] God initiates this relationship between himself and humanity.

In conclusion, the significance of the flood story lies in the preservation of humanity through the instrumentality of one individual. God decided to preserve one particular person, Noah.[20] It was through only one individual that the human line was preserved. The animals were rescued also; each pair was spared to continue the species. This incident reminds us of what took place at Creation: humans and animals existed together.[21] The election of one individual, Noah, made this event possible.

James Daane draws a mission implication from the election of Noah:

> The Noahic covenant has mission implications of first magnitude. We begin with noting the sovereign reaching out on God's part in his mysterious selection of Noah for salvation and service.... A biblical theology of mission must postulate the reality of God's unconditional election and sovereign call. No other dimension of his activity so humbles the people of God.... Divine election is deeply woven into the fabric of 'salvation history' and must be proclaimed as 'good news.'... The essence of the gospel is that Jesus Christ is God's elect (Eph. 3:11). Election must not be construed as God's selectivity whereby some are predestined to eternal life and 'the reprobates' are predestined to eternal life damnation. The gospel must be freely preached as good news for all peoples everywhere or it is not good news at all.[22]

This statement implies that the message of salvation should be shared by elected people. The all-embracing universality of the promise of grace should be made known through people who have experienced this grace. This good news must accompany the message of repentance for sins and the purging of evil thoughts from the heart.

The covenant in Genesis 9:17 clearly demonstrates that 'all flesh, all life on the earth, every living being in the millennia of the history of nature and of humanity is preserved in God's affirmation of his creation.'[23] The covenant of Noah with the 'rainbow' sign is significant of God's salvation and the restoration of humankind.

2.3 Abraham

The story of the fall in Genesis 3 and the flood account in Genesis 9:8-17 describe clearly how human beings have failed and how punishment has

---

[19] Westermann, *Genesis 1-11*, 473.

[20] Westermann, *Genesis 1-11*, 393.

[21] Westermann, *Genesis 1-11*, 55.

[22] James Daane, *The Freedom of God* (Grand Rapids, MI: Eerdmans, 1973), 50.

[23] Westermann, *Genesis 1-11*, 474.

come upon them because of disobedience and sin. However, God still provided hope and an optimistic future for humankind. This implies that he will not give up but will always have a loving heart for the salvation and restoration of his own creation. He not only made covenants with Adam and Noah, but also elected a man who could actually begin fulfilling his purpose of salvation.

Genesis 12:1-3 records the election of Abraham. When God called Abraham he pronounced a 'blessing' on him, his seed, and all the people of the earth.

> I will make you into a great nation
> and I will bless you;
> I will make your name great,
> and you will be a blessing.
> I will bless those who bless you,
> and whoever curses you I will curse;
> And all peoples on earth
> will be blessed through you.

Verse 1 contains a divine command as a test of Abraham's faith: he must leave everything behind to head for an unseen land promised by God. Genesis 22:2 confirms a very similar imperative to Abraham, apparently prefaced by the note that God tests Abraham (v. 1). Going to the designated place requires simple obedience, and an action of submission which brings a great blessing to him. God himself promises 'blessing' upon Abraham which is incidentally the central theme in the covenant of Abraham. Grammatically, the main verbs, 'make', 'bless', 'make great', 'be', 'bless', 'curse', 'finding blessing' are all subordinate to the imperative 'go' (v. 1).[24] Thus, as he goes, these blessings will be bestowed on Abraham.

There are fourfold promises: the promise of a great nation, a great name, divine safekeeping, and being a mediator of blessing.[25] The first promise was that Abraham will become a 'great nation' (v. 1). This promise is repeated in different words in various passages: 'Abraham will surely become a great and powerful nation, and all nations on earth will be blessed through him' (Gen. 18:18). 'Do not be afraid to go down to Egypt, for I will make you into a great nation there' (Gen. 46:3). Exodus 32:10 expresses the closest correspondence: 'Then I will make you into a great nation.' Moses' descendants, those of Abraham, should become a great nation. Thus, God's promise is clear that he will make Abraham a great nation.

---

[24] Wenham, *Genesis 1-15*, 275.
[25] Wenham, *Genesis 1-15*, 275.

The second promise was to 'make your name great' (v. 2). The promise of a great nation and name are 'one of the clearest links between the story of the patriarchs and the history of Israel.'[26] The following sentence, 'and you will be a blessing', confirms and explains why God makes Abraham's name great. Abraham was elected as one of God's favorites upon whom he would bestow blessings. All gifts are to be shared to make others rich.[27] In other words, Abraham had been blessed, for 'he will be a source of blessing to others.'[28]

The third promise was heavenly protection. The early part of verse 3 notes, 'I will bless those who bless you and whoever curses you I will curse.' This implies an intimate relationship between God and Abraham. Physical protection is fully guaranteed. He promised to intervene on Abraham's behalf. All people who bless Abraham will themselves be blessed, but cursed will be the people who curse Abraham. As God commanded Abraham to go to the Promised Land, he assured Abraham with abundant blessings and promises.

The fourth promise continues in the same verse, 'All peoples on earth will be blessed through you.' This was the primary purpose of the entire covenant offered to Abraham. It was a promise of universal blessing to all people, tribes, and nations realized through the chosen man, Abraham. Thus, Abraham was the instrument of God to impart blessings to all different groups of people.[29] This is the first allusion to the centrality of Israel in God's decision to bless the nations. 'There is a note of finality associated with the conduct of any person or people toward Abraham's seed.'[30] Galatians 3:8 confirms this: 'The Scripture foresaw that God would justify the Gentiles by faith, and announced the gospel in advance to Abraham: "All nations will be blessed through you."' Thus, this promise has a redemptive tone which ultimately will be fulfilled through Jesus Christ, 'the Savior of the world' (Jn. 4:42).

Concluding the discussion of the promises, a 'progressive buildup'[31] in Genesis 12:1-3 quickly surfaces:

1) Abraham alone is blessed. → 2) Abraham's name used as a blessing. → 3) Abraham's blessers are blessed. → 4) All families find blessing in Abraham.

---

[26] Westermann, *Genesis 1-11*, 12-36, 37-50

[27] Walter C. Kaiser, *Mission in the Old Testament* (Grand Rapids, MI: Baker, 2000), 18.

[28] H.W. Wolff, 'Das Kerygma des Jahwisten', *EVT* 24 (1964), 73-98.

[29] Kaiser, *Mission in the Old Testament*, 19.

[30] Arthur F. Glasser, *Kingdom and Mission* (Pasadena, CA: Fuller Theological Seminary, School of World Mission, 1989), 58.

[31] Wenham, *Genesis 1-15*, 278.

Walter C. Kaiser states clearly that the promise of blessing coming from God's will counteract the curse. While the entire universe had been put under a curse due to the transgression of Adam and Eve, God had a plan of blessing upon his creatures. The universal scope of this promise is obvious. It is only bestowed by God's grace, not by any human efforts.[32]

Romans 4:13 states that Abraham is the 'heir of the world.' Galatians 3:14 declares, 'He redeemed us in order that the blessing given to Abraham might come to the Gentiles through Christ Jesus, so that by faith we might receive the promise of the Spirit.'

Kaiser further states,

> That one 'Seed' was epitomized through its succession of representatives who acted as earnests or down payments until Christ himself should come in that same line of representatives as both part of that succession and as the final consummation of that to which it pointed. Moreover, all who believed, in all ages, were likewise part of the many of whom the One, Christ, embodied the collective whole.[33]

Therefore, there is a divine purpose for the election of one individual: to bring spiritual blessing on the whole (universally) through the 'Seed.' Abraham and his descendants are chosen to fulfill the significant purpose of God.

2.4 Moses

The background to Moses is found in Exodus 3. The Exodus event is significant in terms of its paramount supernatural manifestation and the deliverance of people by God's mighty hand. Thus, Israel's history begins with this critical experience when the slaves are liberated and changed into a 'self-conscious people.'[34] Moses makes a crucial connection between Abraham and David in this historical event. Obviously, God's promise to Abraham was fulfilled not in his lifetime but through his descendants.

God called Moses at a burning bush on Horeb, the mountain of God. It was a moment of encounter with Yahweh. In revealing his name to Moses, God made a claim over the patriarchs: 'I am the God of your fathers, the God of Abraham, the God of Isaac and the God of Jacob' (Ex. 3:6). The primary purpose of God's calling upon Moses was to rescue his people from their suffering in Egypt. However, Moses had legitimate objections.[35] The first was his own unimportance, 'Who am I?' (v. 11).

---

[32] Kaiser, *Mission in the Old Testament*, 20.

[33] Kaiser, *Mission in the Old Testament*, 20.

[34] Glasser, *Kingdom and Mission*, 69.

[35] Ronald F. Youngblood, *Exodus*, Everyman's Bible Commentary (Chicago, IL: Moody Press, 1983), 33-35.

God's answer was, 'I will be with you' (v. 12). The second was his uncertainty relating to what he should say if his fellow Israelites questioned him as to what God's name was (v. 13). Here the name refers not to God's title but to his nature and character. Yahweh's sufficient answer was, 'I am who I am', 'I will be who I will be.' The third objection was his fear that the Israelites might not believe him or listen to him (Ex. 4:1). God helped Moses to perform three astonishing signs. All these assured Moses to such an extent that he was able to embark on the deliverance of the Israelites from Egypt.

Pharaoh was a religious person. The backdrop to the entire structure of Egyptian veneration and 'animal-worship' was a deep devotion to the mysterious power that holds the world in its control.[36] The exhibition of God's power through 'signs' (Ex. 7:3), 'wonders' (Ex. 7:3) and 'mighty acts of judgments' (Ex. 7:4) was a spectacular way to magnify the identity of the God of the Israelites: his might and power. It was also a means by which God would complete his purpose, as the encounter would harden the heart of Pharaoh (cf. Ex. 4:21). The grip of Egypt on Israel was to be released, but this would happen only through magnificent manifestations of divine power. Pharaoh's heart was hardened in the clash, until the waves of the Red Sea closed over him and his army. No magicians of Egypt could compete with Moses. Thus, redemption was God's ultimate act for his people.

Deliverance from the hand of Pharaoh was not the end of the story. God's specific purpose for the Israelites was revealed only after the deliverance. Exodus 19 describes the Sinai covenant and obligations for Israel. Verses 5-6, together with Genesis 12:1-3 and Isaiah 49:6, are frequently called the Old Testament equivalent to the 'Great Commission.'[37] God's covenants with his people are always 'suzerainty covenants', which means, 'The covenant would impose terms of surrender by the king of a superior power on to the ruler of an inferior power.'[38] It is unilaterally performed by God himself. He is the heavenly King and the Israelites are his human subordinates. Thus, he declared this covenant with his people at Mount Sinai as 'my' (v. 5) covenant. This covenant would be best understood as the consistent development and growth of his covenant with Abraham and his offspring. The divine blessing of the Abrahamic covenant was contingent on obedience and faith (Gen. 17:1, 9; 18:19; 22:18; 26:4-5; Deut. 30:15-20). Likewise, the Sinaitic covenant was conditional. Verse 5 states clearly: 'Now if you obey me fully and keep my covenant, then out of all nations you will be my treasured possession.' This also implies that disobedience will result

---

[36] F.B. Meyer, *Devotional Commentary on Exodus* (Grand Rapids, MI: Kregel, 1978), 107.

[37] Youngblood, *Exodus*, 91.

[38] Youngblood, *Exodus*, 91.

in curses (Deut. 28:15-68) rather than bringing blessing (Deut. 28:1-14).[39] Thus, this covenant came with a heavy obligation, which required perfect obedience in following God's law.

Verses 5-6 contain four significant phrases: 'out of all nations', 'treasured possession', 'a kingdom of priests', and 'a holy nation.' The term 'treasured possession' (Deut. 7:6; 14:2; 26:18; Ps. 135:4; Mal. 3:17) refers to a precious item. 'Although the whole earth' (v. 5) and all things were created by God and belong to him (Gen. 14:19, 22; Ps. 24:1-2), Israel is his extraordinary treasure.

The phrase 'a kingdom of priests' does not occur in any other place in the Old Testament, although Isaiah 61:6 is comparable. Alan Cole notes:

> It is the universal priestly status of Israel to which attention is called. This is all the more understandable in view of the fact that there does not as yet seem to have been any priestly caste within Israel itself. Presumably the basic thought is of a group set apart peculiarly for God's possession and service, with free access to his presence. The thought of acting as God's representative for, and to, the other nations of the world cannot be ruled out. Whether realized at the time or not, this was to be the mission of Israel (cf. the ultimate promise to Abraham in Gen. 12:3). God's particularist choice of Israel has a wider 'universalist' purpose.[40]

Therefore, the Israelites are honored and privileged to be called priests who represent God and interact with the Divine Being. This privilege has a purpose to be fulfilled to the nations.

'A holy nation' implies basically a nation 'set apart' from the other nations. Israel as a 'chosen people' existed as an 'entity' only after the Sinai covenant. The term 'holy' means 'dedicated' to Yahweh without any significant moral implications. However, due to the 'holiness' of God's character there existed a strong moral sense. Eventually, God's holiness was to be a forceful moral stipulation on his people (Lev. 20:7). This consecration of the chosen people, along with the priesthood of the people of God, is underscored repeatedly in the terms of the new covenant (1 Pet. 2:9).[41]

There are commands for the Israelites to practice. Out of the Ten Commandments the first four are associated with God. The rest are concerned with fellow human beings. The first command in verse 3 says, 'You shall have no other gods before me.' The second is in verse 4: 'you shall not make for yourself an idol....' Verse 5, related to verse 4, elaborates on how God feels about his own people: 'I, the Lord your God, am a jealous God.' Thus, the first and second commandments are

---

[39] Youngblood, *Exodus*, 92.

[40] R. Alan Cole, *Exodus: An Introduction and Commentary* (Downers Grove, IL: Inter-Varsity, 1973), 145.

[41] Cole, *Exodus*, 145.

parallel. The expression 'jealous God' implies the complete rationality of God, making 'totalitarian claims' upon his people. He has the right to go through every aspect of each person's private and communal life (Deut. 18:13). The passion of God is his jealous love for his own. Their relationship to him set them apart for a great task. As they obeyed the law, keeping their mind on Yahweh, their 'holy' nature was to take on a moral value as well.[42]

Keeping the Sabbath is the other command (v. 10). Verses 8-10 state, 'Remember the Sabbath day by keeping it holy. Six days you shall labor and do all your work, but the seventh day is a Sabbath to the Lord your God.' The Sabbath should be kept as the holy day of God and the holy people should spend their time in praiseworthy worship (Num. 28:9-10). It is a symbol of separation from other nations as God's very own (Ezek. 20:12, 20). The other commandments are God's instructions on how to live a worthy and exemplary life as God's chosen.

In conclusion, Moses played a great role in leading the people of God from the bondage of slavery. The nation Israel was created during the period of slavery in Egypt, as the fulfilment of God's promise made to Abraham (Gen. 15:13-14). The imposition of commands upon them was for specific reasons. As the chosen people living a holy life, following the commandments was compulsory. Through living a consecrated life, the nations around them would come to discover the God of Israel, who is the Creator of the universe and nations. Their explicit mission was to make God's name and his existence known to the ends of the earth.

2.5 David

The promise that God made to the ancestors of the Israelites was affirmed to David, particularly in his prayer as he responded to the oracle of Nathan (2 Sam. 7:5-11). This prayer was a mixture of 'yielding and insistence' reflecting his faith, and representing in turn 'Israel's prayer.'[43] David was a crucial figure in conquering Jerusalem (2 Sam. 5:6) where God was to have his dwelling place (vv. 13-14). David fulfilled the promise by inheriting the land given to Abraham in Genesis 15:18-21.

The declaration of God through Nathan is the root of the messianic tradition in ancient Israel. The promise apparently dealt with David's son, Solomon, but it further implied the continuation of David's house.[44] Specifically, verse 11 is God's promise to make a 'house', that is, a

---

[42] Glasser, *Kingdom and Mission*, 73.

[43] Robert M. Brown and Elie Wiesel, *Messenger to All Humanity* (Norte Dame, IN: University of Notre Dame Press, 1983), 154.

[44] Walter Brueggemann, *First and Second Samuel*, Interpretation a Bible Commentary for Teaching and Preaching (Louisville, KY: John Knox Press, 1973), 257.

dynasty, out of David and his own descendants (v. 12). Furthermore, the 'Seed' is what David anticipated for God's salvation.[45] The line of David was no longer merely a historical reality but a fundamental element in God's plan of human redemption. A coming One would establish a righteous government. This figure may be concealed in the 'vagaries of history', and may experience obstruction from the 'recalcitrance of injustice and unrighteousness.' However, this coming One would bring justice and righteousness. This oracle through Nathan gives hope to the Israelites and made them trust that the promise would be upheld throughout history by agents of God.[46] This promise was not just one of several but the only one for the salvation of humanity.

2 Samuel 7:18-29 is a long prayer of David, but verses 18-19 particularly include the messianic idea:

Who am I, O Sovereign Lord, and what is my family, that you have brought me this far? And as if this were not enough in your sight, O Sovereign Lord, you have also spoken about the future of the house of your servant. Is this your usual way of dealing with man, O Sovereign Lord?

According to Kaiser, most English versions translate these verses differently from the original rendering of the text. The last clause of verse 19 is usually translated as, 'Is this your usual way of dealing with man?', while Kaiser renders it, 'and this is the charter for humanity, O Lord Yahweh.'[47] Kaiser further points out,

And what did David have reference to by his use of 'this' in 'and this is the charter for humanity'? The antecedent can be nothing less than the substance of the oracle that had just been given to him by the prophet Nathan. 'This' refers in context to the revelation David had just been given about the 'Seed.'[48]

This prediction was to make his great plans known and reveal hidden secrets of the future to his servants. Through the 'Seed' of David, all humanity would be able to come to the salvation of Christ.

Here the 'charter' is identical to 'law' and 'decree' by which God accomplishes his scheme for all human beings. Thus, the 'law', which is the Word of God, is intended to teach all humanity. The promise of dynasty and kingdom is connected with the future promise of God.[49]

One should acknowledge that the oracle of Nathan with the absolute promise to David is the most acute theological proclamation in the Old Testament. This announcement of a royal line is a radical separation from

---

[45] Kaiser, *Mission in the Old Testament*, 23-24.
[46] Brueggemann, *First and Second Samuel*, 257-58.
[47] Kaiser, *Mission in the Old Testament*, 26.
[48] Kaiser, *Mission in the Old Testament*, 27.
[49] Kaiser, *Mission in the Old Testament*, 27.

the conditional feature of the Mosaic 'if' (cf. Ex. 19:4-6). The historical records make us aware of the actuality of judgments and conditions. However, here God's unrestricted promise is revealed through Nathan's oracle of 'nevertheless.' This already signals the unconditional nature of the gospel.[50]

The oracle of Nathan and David's prayer indicate clearly God's plan, which actually promised a 'Seed' through the chosen servants of God. The 'Seed' will be flesh and blood to save humanity.

2.6 Jesus Christ (Messiah)

God's mission to save fallen humanity is fully recognized in Jesus, the Messiah. God's creation was devastated by the fall. However, God promised the 'Seed' for the redemption of fallen humanity (Gen. 3:15). The covenants God made in different periods of Israel's history are God's sovereign and passionate acts of grace and love for the whole of humanity. David Shank well describes historical events in Israel:

> The movement in history has been from creation to humanity, followed by alienation from God and his purposes; from salvaged but alienated humanity to Abraham and Israel, for all of humanity; from unfaithful Israel to a faithful remnant, for all Israel; from the remnant to the one 'Anointed'—the Messiah. According to the prophets, when Messiah comes, he is for the remnant, the remnant is for all of Israel, Israel is for all of humanity, and humanity is for all of the earth as creation. Henceforth, Israel in the midst of foreign oppression, exile, dispersion, and the return of many to Zion is constantly confronted with the bitter facts of that yet-unrealized messianic fulfilment.[51]

John declares, 'The Word became flesh and dwelt among us' (1:14) implying that God has accomplished a new way of entrance for fellowship. It is the 'particularity of the incarnation' that fulfills the 'universal validity' of Lord, Jesus Christ.[52]

2.6.1 SUFFERING SERVANT

The suffering Servant is the anointed one into whom God endows his Spirit (Is. 42:1). That is the Messiah. He will 'bring justice to the nations' (Is. 42:1), 'till he establishes justice on earth' (Is. 42:4). This depicts the mission of Yahweh for the nations and his unlimited activity for the

---

[50] Brueggemann, *First and Second Samuel*, 259.

[51] David A. Shank, 'Jesus the Messiah: Messianic Foundation of Mission', in Wilbert R. Shenk (ed), *The Transfiguration of Mission: Biblical, Theological, and Historical Foundations* (Scottdale, PA: Herald, 1993), 37-82.

[52] Wilbert R. Shenk, 'The Relevance of a Messianic Missiology for Mission Today', in Wilbert R. Shenk (ed), *The Transfiguration of Mission: Biblical, Theological, and Historical Foundations* (Scottdale, PA: Herald Press, 1993), 17-36.

salvation of humanity. Thus, the Messiah will be the true light to the nations. The Israelites, physical and spiritual (that is, Christians), become an instrument to partake in the mission of the suffering Servant.

In order to accomplish this mission the Messiah is expected to suffer. Isaiah 49:7 and 50:6 note that the Servant will be scorned, disdained, and spat upon. The suffering Servant is indeed wounded, bruised, chastised, oppressed, afflicted as the sacrificial offering for sin.[53]

Isaiah 53:3-5 describes the plight of the suffering Servant.

> He was despised and rejected by men, a man of sorrows, and familiar with suffering. Like one from whom men hide their faces he was despised, and we esteemed him not. Surely he took up our infirmities and carried our sorrows, yet we considered him stricken by God, smitten by him, afflicted. But he was pierced for our transgressions, he was crushed for our iniquities, the punishment that brought us peace was upon him, and by his wounds we are healed.

Christians believe that whenever the world suffers, God is also suffering with it.[54] People in different parts of the world encounter diverse kinds of suffering. For example, children in Ethiopia are starving, Cambodia was known as the 'killing fields', the Philippines suffer natural disasters (an average of twenty-two typhoons visit this country before traveling to neighboring Asian nations). The suffering Servant joins the suffering of people with compassion and passion. 'God is not an apathetic being.' 'God is pathetic' as he joins the suffering of people.[55]

Obviously, the final word for believers is not suffering but hope. Authentic hope is moving to 'hope-in-the-midst-of-adversity', resting secure in God's coming victory over the evil world.[56] We realize and proclaim that the Servant's last triumph has already penetrated the present age with its beam, however 'opaque these rays may be and however much they may be contradicted by the empirical reality of adversity and suffering.'[57] In the mean time, we encounter countless agonizing moments and at times may feel victimized. But, believers trust in God's ultimate triumph and in this hope we continue our mission.

The substitutionary suffering and death are the duty of the Servant as 'a guilt offering for sin (Is. 53:10) made', 'for the transgression of my

---

[53] Shank, 'Jesus the Messiah', 60.

[54] C.H. Ratschow, 'Ist Gott angesichts der Leiden in der Welt zu rechtfertigen?', in C.H. Ratschow (ed), *Von den Wandlungen Gottes* (Berlin: Walter de Gruyter, 1986), 176-79; Johannes Triebel, 'Leiden als Thema der Missionstheologie', *Jahrbuch Mission* 20 (1988), 8-15.

[55] Shusaku Endo, *Silence*, trans. W. Johnston (London: Peter Owen, 1976), 297.

[56] Christian Beker, *Suffering and Hope: The Biblical Vision and the Human Predicament* (Philadelphia, PA: Fortress, 1987), 84.

[57] Christian Beker, *Paul and Apostle: The Triumph of God in Life and Thought* (Philadelphia, PA: Fortress, 1982), 58.

people' (Is. 53:8), he 'bears the sin of many and made intercession for the transgressors' (Is. 53:12). The Servant's victory is a result of the total surrender of his life even to death.[58] His glorification is an outcome of his faithfulness in spite of rebuff, torment, and death. The Servant 'will be raised and lifted up and highly exalted' (Is. 52:13).

2.6.2 UNRESTRICTED MISSION

One of the features of Christ's mission is inclusiveness: embracing different levels of people, the poor and the rich, spiritual and unspiritual, and both the neglected and accepted. His mission is to break down walls of animosity, to cross borders between groups,[59] accepting unforgivable people and different ethnic groups. Luke 7:36-50 tells about a woman whose life has been sinful and is accused by people around her.

> Now one of the Pharisees invited Jesus to have dinner with him, so he went to the Pharisee's house and reclined at the table. When a woman who had lived a sinful life in that town learned that Jesus was eating at the Pharisee's house, she brought an alabaster jar of perfume, and as she stood behind him at his feet weeping, she began to wet his feet with her tears. Then she wiped them with her hair, kissed them and poured perfume on them. When the Pharisee who had invited him saw this, he said to himself, 'If this man were a prophet, he would know who is touching him and what kind of woman she is—that she is a sinner.' Jesus answered him, 'Simon, I have something to tell you.'

Jesus taught using a simple parable so Simon's stereotypical mind could be challenged. He counter-questioned Simon, 'Do you see this woman?' He contrasted the two individuals. She honored Christ by wetting his feet with her tears and wiping his feet with her hair. Furthermore, she kissed Christ when he entered the room. Not only that, she poured expensive and precious perfume on his feet. However, Simon did nothing of significance in welcome.

This story reveals two stances of mind and heart. Simon feels no need for repentance and thus forgiveness. On the contrary, the woman considers herself not worthy of facing Jesus. She humbles herself and shows affection to him. This attitude pleases him and consequently she receives forgiveness. Francis of Assisi confesses that 'There is nowhere a more wretched and a more miserable sinner than I.'[60] It is correct to say that the 'greatest sin is to be conscious of no sin; but a sense of need will

---

[58] Shank, 'Jesus the Messiah', 37-82.

[59] David J. Bosch, *Transforming Mission: Paradigm Shifts in Theology of Mission* (Maryknoll, NY: Orbis, 1993), 29.

[60] William Barclay, *The Gospel of Luke*, Daily Study Bible Series (Philadelphia, PA: Westminster, 1975), 95.

open the door to the forgiveness of God, because God is love, and love's greatest glory is to be needed.'[61]

Christ's earthly ministry is not restricted to power demonstrations and teaching but includes transforming the minds and hearts of people. His radically inclusive attitude of receiving the woman must have impacted the people of his day.

III. Conclusion

God's plan for human salvation was set forth from the very beginning of human history. After the fall God's promise of posterity, the promise of the 'Seed', was given to Adam and Eve. The Bible clearly records human failure through transgression. Noah was the righteous man through whom God's provision of salvation was promised. God continued to elect people who would be able to take part in the fulfilment of salvation. Abraham was called to leave his homeland with divine assurance from God. Divine protection was also guaranteed. Abraham's obedience in going to the Promised Land was a pleasing act of obedience in the eyes of God. Through Moses the Israelites were rescued from Egyptian slavery. God intended to set apart these people for the purpose of the *Missio Dei,* the universal mission of God. David received an oracle from Yahweh through Nathan, which included the promise of the 'Seed', the Messiah, who would come through David's lineage. Finally, the Messiah came into the world to save sinners. He offered himself for the sins of the world. This suffering Servant took up the cross to die as a living sacrifice. The *Missio Dei* of salvation is eventually fulfilled through Jesus Christ, and the mission of God continues through bearers of the gospel and the church. The good news of the gospel will continuously be proclaimed to the ends of the earth until the Lord returns.

---

[61] Barclay, *The Gospel of Luke,* 95.

Miracle in Papasok

March to Papasok

Papasok is a village located in the mountains, an eight hour drive from Baguio City, the Philippines' summer capital. To go to this village, one needs to drive the Halsema Highway, a major road in terrible condition. It is constantly damaged by landslides, and suffers from poor road construction. The slash-and-burn technique farmers use for growing crops on hills and mountains naturally washes off the topsoil and covers the road. Ordinary cars are not able to drive along this road which is between 1,500 to 2,000 feet above sea level. Moreover, the deadly earthquake in July of 1990 shook the mountains greatly, leaving the road in even worse condition. Because of this, many people are isolated and confined to their own villages until access to another place is provided.

When we hike to the mountains, we usually stop at a restaurant in a bus stop in Sayangan, one of the villages along the highway. The restaurant has many 'exotic' dishes, including roasted dog meat. This restaurant is particularly enjoyed by the people. We drive further north to our destination, Papasok. Upon arriving, we see cogoon houses, a traditional Kankana-ey house made of rice straw. The surface of the cogoon houses is black because of the smoke from the fires in the kitchen. The road soon shrinks to a size much too small for cars to pass through, so we have to park our car about a forty-five minute walk away from the village. Children and grown-ups, rush to welcome us.

Who Are They?

The town consists of twenty houses and people are content with their simple and humble lives. Because it begins to get dark around seven o'clock, they go to sleep early and wake up early in the morning. No available electricity shapes this lifestyle. The church members, knowing our exhaustion, boil water with ginger and mix it with coffee. We are told that this drink is very native and can be found only in the mountain villages. We add several spoonfuls of brown sugar, enough to make it hard for one to distinguish the taste from coffee. After a time of rest, we happily walk to the church where the members have been waiting for us since early afternoon. Gospel songs and hymns are sung to God.

These simple people are isolated by the growing and modern world. City people are hesitant to visit them and even believers resist traveling for ministry. To some, these humble people are less than human. This is probably why the people of Papasok are always so excited to see people from a different place.

Only twenty-five years ago those who dwell here were typical Igorots[1] — worshippers of deceased ancestors. In the past, when a family member fell sick, had an inexplicable dream, or saw anything as simple as a strange looking bird flying over them, they would immediately seek the help of a village priest. These priests are typically known as a *mambunong*, and are sought out to explain any unusual experience.

A consultation may reveal something similar to the following. The *mambunong* may declare that the dead spirit of a grandfather is not content with the family's attention and is angry to the point of causing terrible things to happen. Prescriptions from the priest for soothing the spirits are very costly. Traditionally a sacrifice is demanded, maybe a few perfect native pigs. The priest decides the due date, which they call *canyao*. The priest who conducts the *canyao*[2] holds the highest spiritual authority and power and is the final decision-maker. The count of sacrificial animals begins at one, then three, five and progresses much higher in number. The more sacrifices to be offered the higher the count. The rule of ritual is set, so that no one can refuse it. Therefore, families are compelled to perform these rituals even to the point of borrowing money from a friend or relative.

God's Sovereign Will

The story of God's salvation in this village (it is his story) begin when the good news was brought by a pastor and his wife. As strangers from another village, the residents hesitantly extended a welcome. One evening, the pastor invited the people for a gathering. One of the hosts lit a gas lamp; a rarity the people see only a few times in a year. The lamp worked better as an invitation than the invitation by the pastor. This illiterate pastor started by telling the story of Jesus Christ which he had just heard from an evangelist. The listeners were particularly interested in the Genesis story of creation and were enlightened in their souls. The villagers had always been taught that the spirits whom they honored and worshipped made the entire universe. However, the creation account, told in a natural way, instead of using formal homiletics, helped to open their

---

[1] Igorot refers to the mountain tribal people in the northern Luzon in the Philippines.

[2] Canyao is a traditional ritual which has been practiced throughout the generations. Ancestor worshippers in the mountains frequently refer to the spirits through Canyao when a member of the family is sick and terrified by a horrible dream, and some other occasions.

spirits to the Spirit of God. Truly, the Holy Spirit assisted the pastor as he led the people. After that, the pastor regularly visited the village with the gospel in mind. He drew more and more people every time he visited, with the villagers eagerly listening to his intriguing stories.

But this is not the end of the story. The pastor, full of knowledge, came back to the village during the dry season with a young man named Reynaldo, who had dropped out of Bible school. The pastor freely expressed himself and became more energetic as he led the Bible study for the regular attendees. His unpretentious yet serious way of telling Bible stories soon attracted many non-Christians from nearby villages. During his time, a couple named Badol drew his attention, as they became increasingly interested. The wife was very shy and bashful, while her husband was more on the quiet side. Soon after this time, the pastor heard of the death of the couple's two children because of a high fever. It is very common for children to die of something as insignificant as a fever because of their weak immune systems. Understandably, this incident left them with great sorrow and a life-long heartache. Knowing this, the pastor, out of love, began to pray that the couple would bear more children. Typically, the mountain tribal people have many children, on average between ten to twelve. Most people found his prayers for offspring quite unnecessary. Amazingly, God answered the pastor's prayer and, in two years, the couple bore two more children. While the pastor was awestruck, the villagers were not amazed at all.

A Grief of the Lost Sons

One night, the Badols did not attend the Bible study. The pastor had planned to minister to them.

Out of concern, he asked his host,

'Did you see the Badols tonight?'

'No,' he replied, 'they did not come tonight.'

Immediately, the pastor rushed out of his room and searched for their house. While he was looking for Badol's house, he met a villager.

'Have you seen Walse-en Badol?', the pastor asked.

'As a matter of fact I have,' the villager replied, 'They took their two children to a town hospital because of high fever.'

He continued, 'They are away from home, and will return perhaps tomorrow.'

Reluctantly, the pastor returned to his room and tried to fall asleep. Suddenly, noisy wails from a woman sounded from nearby. The noise spread all over the village. The pastor soon saw the Badols approaching him with tears in their eyes. They told him the sad news of the death of their two children. Beginning that night, an epidemic had swept the village, striking the children in particular. Even to this day, many children are victims of this sickness. Sadly, no medication was available for treatment. Many undernourished children died because of this malicious epidemic that started as a fever.

'Where are the bodies?'

'They are near the village entrance. If you would not mind, please bury the bodies for us; I will accompany you.'

The pastor quietly nodded.

Imposition of Traditional Custom

In this sad and emotional time, there were quiet talks among the villagers. The Badol's attitude towards the pastor's help struck many of them the wrong way. Obviously, the couple has to follow the traditional ways for a funeral, passed down from their ancestors! A traditional funeral is accompanied by an animal sacrifice. If anyone violates this rule it is believed that a terrible curse will be upon the family from an ancestral spirit. Also, a village priest or an elder must conduct the funeral.

Badol took the lifeless bodies of his children to his house. No one in the village, not even his relatives, was willing to help him because of his choice to conduct the funeral non-traditionally. His decision not only shocked the villagers. When he prepared to bury the bodies, his relatives tried their best to stop him from following the 'wrong' way of conducting the funeral. Some infuriated elders cursed him and swore. 'Is it not enough to lose two children?' 'Do you wish to lose more children?', they cried. In fact, Badol's father-in-law argued with his daughter and son-in-law because of his fear that the spirits may attack his daughter. Indeed, the situation became chaotic.

Badol did not respond. He calmly left the loud crowd, showing his determination. This caused the people to cease arguing and to stop discussing the matter. The villagers scattered to their own places. Eventually, the dead were buried without controversy.

Soon after, Badol left home to do errands, leaving his wife alone. According to tribal tradition, for a certain period of time following the funeral, family members should refrain from being involved in any daily activities and stay home. Mrs Badol, too, carried on and worked at home, ignoring the customs. This was considered risky by their neighbors. This couple deviated in two important ways: they neglected to perform the funeral according to traditional customs, and then broke a second custom by working. It was believed that their misbehavior would anger the spirits and bring further life-threatening conflicts. While others carefully watched to see when his wife would become ill, Badol safely returned with gospel tracks from his pastor.

Badol grew in faith, while, unknowingly, his pastor was praying for him. His prayer was that Badol would become a leader for the congregation. He listened well and grew in faith. God answered the pastor's prayer. Badol's wife joined him in faith and ministry. This was an important issue. Unless a divine power intervened, abandoning one's cultural practices was unimaginable. Such dedication and faith is something we can all learn.

The Badols continued to prove their faith even after this incident, as they conducted Sunday services in their small house. The village people who had seen the protection of the Christian God upon this family became convinced that the God whom the Badols believed in was stronger than their gods. This conviction drew them to join the worship services and helped to lead many to Christ. When babies were sick, their parents would bring them for healing prayer. To the Badols' amazement, the number of newcomers increased every Sunday, most coming without a personal invitation from them. God, indeed, performed a great miracle in that place and the entire village came to the Lord within a few years. The Badols' unswerving determination to follow biblical principles was essential for the salvation of their village.

CHAPTER 2

Light: A Missiological Reading

I. Introduction

The concept of light in the Bible has rich missiological implications. For instance, Isaiah 49:6 reads, '...I will make you a light for the Gentiles, that you may bring my salvation to the ends of the earth.' This implies that the Israelites have a task of witnessing for God to the world. In the New Testament, John 1:9 reads, 'I [Jesus] am the light.' The Messiah who brought the hope of salvation into the darkness is, indeed, the true light. Matthew 5:14 and 8:12 note that believers are the light of the world. The term 'light' apparently contains an implication that the children of God have a significant role in the world. In short, people who have freely received the gospel of salvation, or seen the light (Is. 9:2) should reach out to the heathen, or to be a light to others.

This study focuses on the concept of light as found primarily in the book of Isaiah. The development of the concept is further traced in the New Testament. This biblical study is done from a missiological perspective.

II. Light in the Old Testament

2.1 Israel: The Servant of God

Isaiah 41:8 notes that God has chosen Israel from the day of Abraham and given the people their historical existence (cf. Is. 44:2, 21). The expression, 'my servant', is a word of grace. It is clear that the status of Israel is simply the result of God's action. To be the servant of the Lord is to live in faith that one's future is safe in the purpose of God.[1]

In Isaiah, the words 'Israel, my servant' is given a specific role. This statement is often found in the context of a dispute between Yahweh and the gods of the nations to determine sovereignty.[2] The servant Israel has

---

[1] James Luther Mays, *Ezekiel, Second Isaiah*, Proclamation Commentaries (Philadelphia, PA: Fortress, 1978), 86.

[2] Mays, *Ezekiel, Second Isaiah*, 86.

)f proving Yahweh's lordship to the world by
.1's word and deeds (Is. 44:26). In playing this role,
, be a messenger whom the Lord sends (Is. 42:19).
__picts Israel as the servant in whom God will be glorified
__uring the high calling of the servant.

In Isaiah 42-53, the servant of God can refer to either an individual or
a group of people.[3] In the Old Testament the term is specifically used to
refer to individuals who God has chosen, such as Abraham, Moses or
David.[4] The same expression is employed of prophets (1 Kgs. 18:36). In
all cases, each individual was called to fulfill a specific task.

The book of Isaiah calls the people of Israel the servant of Yahweh,
which becomes an example of his special way of personifying the nation
as a single individual. This designation is often found in salvation oracles
(e.g., Is. 41:8-10) to remind the hearers that their special relationship with
Yahweh continues.

Isaiah 49:3 reads, 'And he said to me, "you are my servant, Israel, in
whom I shall be glorified."' In another scripture the same idea appears,
'"You are my witnesses," declares the Lord, "and my servant whom I
have chosen"' (Is. 43:10-11). R.N. Whybray attests that Israel as a nation
is referred to as Yahweh's 'servant' or 'slave' (*'ebed*).[5] God had a
definite purpose when he chose his elected servant Israel to build a
relationship with the nations.[6]

What does it mean to be the servant of God? George A. Knight points
out two future roles for Israel: 1) to re-establish the tribes of Jacob, and to
restore Israel, as preserved in exile in Babylon; and 2) to become a light
to the nations so that Yahweh's salvation may be known to the ends of the
earth.[7] Israel is to become God's instrument in the building of the
relationship with the nations so that Yahweh's name may be known (Is.
49:6). According to Isaiah 42:1-4, the servant has a responsibility to
bring God's judgment or justice (*mishpat*) to the nations implying that
Yahweh alone is the judge among the nations. The servant is God's
representative to set matters right in history, bringing God's rule, order,
and truth out of confusion and falsehood. To accomplish this task, the
servant would be distinguished not by employing the words or deeds of
earthly kings but by offering right instruction to the people of the world.[8]

---

[3] John L. McKenzie, *Second Isaiah*, Anchor Bible (Garden City, NY: Doubleday,
1968), xiii.

[4] Glasser, *Kingdom and Mission*, 69.

[5] R.N. Whybray, *The Second Isaiah*, Old Testament Guides (Sheffield: JSOT Press,
1983), 65.

[6] Mays, *Ezekiel, Second Isaiah*, 87.

[7] George A. Knight, *Isaiah 40-66: Servant Theology*, International Theological
Commentary (Edinburgh/Grand Rapids, MI: Handsel/Eerdmans, 1984), 130.

[8] Mays, *Ezekiel, Second Isaiah*, 87.

However, the servant Israel lost their hope in exile, which came as a result of their unfaithfulness to the covenant relationship with Yahweh. Israel abandoned the One who had called them and were engaged with other gods through the centuries (Is. 48:1). However, even during the exile in Babylon God gave Israel two parallel assignments. Firstly, they were to live as a people of God (Jer. 29:5, 6) and, secondly, they were to serve their captors (Jer. 29:7). Particular focus should be given to the second: the responsibility the exiles have to seek the peace (*shalom*) and comfort of the city of their exile, and to pray to God on its behalf. In the Old Testament, the meaning of shalom is comprehensive, representing wholeness, well-being, a satisfactory condition, body health and so on.[9] Thus, if a person or a nation has shalom then no lack exists in any aspect; there is total harmony. Therefore, it is truly a gift of Yahweh.

After generations of captivity, God restored Israel from the bondage of suffering and renewed their calling as the servant of God. How did God demonstrate his restoring work to his people? He showed his mercy toward them in consolation and encouragement:

Comfort, comfort my people, says your God. Speak tenderly to Jerusalem and proclaim to her that her hard service has been completed that her sin has been paid for, that she has received from the Lord's hand double for all her sins (Is. 40:1-2).

This prophetic proclamation signals the turning point in Israel's fortunes. It implies that its suffering time of servitude is over and its iniquity is pardoned through divine forgiveness.[10] This was good news; hardship will end. In fact, God intends to rescue and to restore them as the promise of comfort implies. It clearly shows that Israel's time of consolation or comfort has come and God is about to use the people in spite of their past rebellion. The preparation for this already took place even while Israel was suffering in Babylon.[11] Indeed, the time of suffering prepared and equipped them to be used as God's instrument for the redemption of the whole world.

Yahweh had confidently chosen his servant Israel declaring,

Be silent before me, you islands! Let the nations renew their strength! Let them come forward and speak; let us meet together at the place of judgment. Who has stirred up one from the east, calling him in righteousness to his service? He hands nations over to him and subdues kings before him. He turns them to dust with his sword, to windblown chaff with his bow.... I, the Lord—with the first of them and with the last—I am he (Is. 41:1-4).

---

[9] Glasser, *Kingdom and Mission*, 99.

[10] Claus Westermann, *Isaiah 40-66*, Old Testament Library, trans. David M.G. Stalker (Philadelphia, PA: Westminster, 1969), 35.

[11] Knight, *Isaiah 40-66*, 132.

Yahweh proclaims in Isaiah 41:4 that he is the first and the last. God's eternity becomes the grounds for humans to put an absolute trust in him. God alone holds universal history. Divine eternity is expressed in the history of Israel.

God has demonstrated his power over other nations. Nothing would prevent the servant's success because the Almighty God is Israel's strong helper. God would fulfill his will of bringing salvation as well as 'judgment' (or 'justice') to the nations. Also, the presence of God's Spirit given to the servant enabled Israel to carry out the assigned task (Is. 41:2-3). Now the servant was aware that his primary task was to make Yahweh's glory known (Is. 49:4).

Israel is reminded that Yahweh's call as his servant came even before Israel was born (Is. 49:1-3). God spoke to them again confirming his original word (Is. 49:1-3). Israel was to revive the stricken nations and to manifest Yahweh's sovereignty manifested in the whole earth.

2.2 Light of the World

God formed the light and he himself is the light (Is. 45:7; 60:3). The One who created the universe and the light calls the nation Israel to be a light to the nations.

> I, the Lord, have called you in righteousness; I will take hold of your hand. I will keep you and will make you to be a covenant for the people and a light for the Gentiles, to open eyes that are blind, to free captives from prison and to release from the dungeon those who sit in darkness (Is. 42:6-7).

God, giving solemn assurance, confirms Israel in this special calling through the covenant (Gen. 15:7-21). They are to be assured that God has guaranteed their life, well-being, and peace.[12] Based on the assurance of this covenant, God reminds them of their commission as he makes them a light to the nations. In other words, through the faithful obedience of Israel, God is to prove himself to be truly God and to be acknowledged as the Lord and Savior of the world. In addition, his glory and praise will be manifested through his saving work of Israel (Is. 42:8).

Isaiah 49:6 states that Israel was to be the 'light' to the Gentiles to bring the salvation of Yahweh to the ends of the earth. God called Israel even from her mother's womb (Is. 49:1, cf. 'a light to the people' in Is. 51:4). According to Whybray,[13] this call is associated with God's expressed will (*torah*) and his universal rule (*mishpat*). That is, the nations of the world have an obligation to accept Yahweh's sovereignty and, as a

---

[12] John Scullion, *Isaiah 40-66*, Old Testament Message 12 (Wilmington, DL: Michael Glazier, 1982), 43.

[13] Whybray, *The Second Isaiah*, 75.

consequence, God will free the nations from their slavery to false gods and beliefs. This salvation of Yahweh will be mediated by Israel (Is. 49:7).

Now God urges Israel to undertake his role as a witness.

> Lead out those who have eyes but are blind, who have ears but are deaf. All the nations gather together and the peoples assemble. Which of them foretold this and proclaimed to us the former things? Let them bring in their witnesses to prove they were right, so that others may hear and say, 'It is true.' 'You are my witnesses,' declares the Lord, 'and my servant whom I have chosen, so that you may know and believe me and understand that I am he. Before me no god was formed, nor will there be one after me' (Is. 43:8-10).

God radically transformed Israel and exclaimed, 'You are my witness.' His people who were once blind can now see through God's fulfilled promise and they become the witnesses of God's unique saving power to the nations of the world. God attempted to bring deaf and dumb Israel to his court in the presence of all the nations. In spite of Israel's restoration, Israel was shameful in their deafness and dumbness.

God intends to draw the nations to himself to recount how he acted in the days of Moses. God brought them through the waters of the Red Sea and made his covenant through Moses (Ex. 14:26-30; 24:1-4). He also recalls that it is he who led them to the land which was not even their possession and who gave them the land as a gift (Is. 6:6-8). This all happened so that Israel would trust and believe in Yahweh so that ultimately they would be a witness of God to the nations as they serve as a proof of the existence of God.[14]

God had called Israel from the beginning and expanded their mission to include the nations (Is. 49:6). The servant's purpose, however, is more than witnessing God's deeds to the nations. It is to bring salvation to them through declaring their own experience of Yahweh's saving power.[15]

This announcement by Yahweh is intended to be uplifting, by assuring them that the work is more significant than they could have thought it to be. God's plan does not stop at the restoration of the scattered Israelites to their homeland and rebuilding of the nation, but is fully realized only when Yahweh's rule is established throughout the world. Isaiah 49:6 may signify that Yahweh's coming victory over Babylon may be one way to convince the nations of Yahweh's kingship so that they would submit to his rule.[16]

---

[14] Knight, *Isaiah 40-66*, 65.

[15] Mays, *Ezekiel, Second Isaiah*, 89.

[16] Whybray, *The Second Isaiah*, 139.

As 'the light of Israel comes, Yahweh's glory rises up' (Is. 60:1). Here the light and glory are parallel.[17] As Israel becomes the light to the world, God's glory will shine. The people in darkness are promised light beaming upon them. The light of Zion will prevail over the darkness resting upon the rest of the world (Is. 60:2-3). Israel was chosen as God's instrument to display to the nations his universal sovereignty and the total salvation of humankind.

III. Light in the New Testament

John 1:9 declares, 'Jesus is the true light.' Throughout God's revelation, only partial lights existed though God's servants like Moses and John the Baptist (Jn. 5:35). As Jesus is the Creator of the world, the Redeemer of humankind, and the saving presence of God in the world, he alone can connect himself with a diminished world (Jn. 3:33) as the light.

3.1 The Mission of John the Baptist

As a light to his own people, John the Baptist declared the Kingdom of God. The Israelites, God's chosen, needed to hear the good news of the kingdom prior to the Gentiles. In such an urgent situation, the role of John the Baptist was critical. He proclaimed primarily judgment: 'The axe is laid to the root of the trees' (Mt. 3:10). He particularly denounced the religious leaders as vipers, and announced that confidence in one's descendency from Abraham was of no value (Mt. 3:7-9). He attempted to make ready the way of the Savior's coming who 'takes away the sins of the world' (Jn. 1:29). He will also judge the nation of Israel, and baptize the penitent with the Holy Spirit (Mt. 3:11, 12). Instantly, Matthew's thoughts were drawn towards the statement, 'The kingdom of heaven is at hand' (Mt. 3:2). As Ezekiel had assured the purification and spiritual transformation of his nation (36:22-36), the time for spiritual repentance had arrived. Thus, the proclamation of an urgent need for repentance was John's primary work in bringing renewal upon his people.

3.2 Jesus' Mission among the Gentiles

Jesus himself said twice that he is the light of the world (Mt. 8:12; 9:5). He also affirmed this among his followers in the Sermon on the Mount: 'You are the light to the world' (Mt. 5:14). While he was on the earth he demonstrated how to live as the light: to release people from the darkness of sin and the bondage of evil, and set people, both Jews and Gentiles,

---

[17] Westermann, *Isaiah 40-66*, 358.

free from sin (Jn. 3:16). His mission perspective was never confined only to his own people, but to the entire human race.

The New Testament reveals the extent of Jesus' mission to the Gentiles. Several Gospel accounts may suffice. The first example of the extended scope of his mission to the Gentiles is found in the Gospel of Matthew:

> Leaving that place, Jesus withdrew to the region of Tyre and Sidon. A Canaanite woman from that vicinity came to him, crying out, 'Lord, Son of David, have mercy on me! My daughter is suffering terribly from demon-possession.' Jesus did not answer a word. So his disciples came to him and urged him, 'Send her away, for she keeps crying out after us.' He answered, 'I was sent only to the lost sheep of Israel.' The woman came and knelt before him. 'Lord, help me,' she said. He replied, 'It is not right to take the children's bread and toss it to their dogs.' 'Yes Lord,' she said, 'but even the dogs eat the crumbs that fall from their master's table.' Then Jesus answered, 'Woman, you have great faith! Your request is granted.' And her daughter was healed from that very hour (Mt. 15:21-28).

The woman's faith is far greater than any in the 'house of Israel.' Jesus placed high value on her faith. He responded to her because of her accurate and insistent replies to his questions and his commendation of her faith brought instant healing by a word alone.[18]

Another example is the demonstration of his healing power for a servant of a Gentile centurion (Mt. 8:5-13). When Jesus questioned the centurion, 'Shall I come and heal him?', he responded to Jesus, 'Just say the word, and my servant will be healed.' Having been amazed at this statement, Jesus exclaimed, 'With no one in Israel have I found such faith.' Matthew stresses the expanded concept of the people of God. In the preceding verses, he indicates that the membership is not limited exclusively to the Israelites. 'Whoever believes and has faith in him would be included in this privilege' (Mt. 8:11).[19]

This is apparently contrary to the Jewish purity laws and rituals, which separated Gentiles from Jews. Jesus' encounter with the Canaanite woman clearly demonstrates the wider scope of 'kingdom membership.' In spite of tight traditional laws, Jesus succeeded in ministering to the Gentile crowds who 'glorified the God of Israel' (Mt. 15:31).[20] The crucial fault of the Jews was their rejection of God's Messiah, which resulted in God's rejection of Israel.[21] Matthew's position is that God has transferred the Kingdom of Heaven to another nation (Mt. 21:43). Jesus spoke of the

---

[18] R.T. France, *Matthew: Evangelist and Teacher* (Grand Rapids, MI: Zondervan, 1989), 234.

[19] Robert H. Gundry, *Matthew: A Commentary on His Literary and Theological Art* (Grand Rapids, MI: Eerdmans, 1982), 141.

[20] France, *Matthew*, 234.

[21] Stephen F. Hre Kio, 'Understanding and Translating "Nation" in Matthew 28:19', *Bible Translator* 41 (1990), 230-38.

replacement by 'another nation' in the parables in Matthew 21 and 22. In Jesus' parable of the invitation to the wedding feast, complete fairness is demonstrated. 'Both good and bad' are invited. Thus, the ground was well prepared; anyone may come to the feast.[22] The implication of this parable is that the blessing the Lord has prepared is not for Israel alone but for the Gentiles as well.

Jesus came to Israel precisely because his mission concerned the whole world. His announcement of salvation to Israel and his vicarious death is an act of service to the Gentiles also. Both take place in order that the incorporation of the Gentiles into the Kingdom of God might be possible.[23]

Thus, no matter how much Jewish people attempted to prevent Jesus from ministering to the Gentiles, his task of spreading the gospel to the world continued. Even though the mission of Jesus and the disciples was initially restricted to the Jews (Mt. 10:5-6, 23), the good news was soon to be preached to the Gentiles (Mt. 24:14). Therefore, there shall be but one banquet: one representation of the universal character of the Kingdom of God.

3.3 Good News for the Gentiles

The purpose of Israel as God's witness and light to the nations (Is. 43:10; 44:8) continued in Jesus on the earth. But after his death, the Holy Spirit was sent by both the Father and the Son to further Jesus' witness and work in the world (Jn. 15:26). Finally, his chosen disciples were sent to accomplish his mission as co-workers with the Holy Spirit (Jn. 17:18).

The close relation between God and Israel is expressed in that 'you are my witnesses' (Is. 49:6). Jesus used the same words to his apostles: 'You shall be my witness' (Acts 1:8). The heralds of the gospel are described as being a light to the Gentiles, bearing God's salvation to the uttermost parts of the earth.[24]

3.3.1 PETER'S OPENNESS TO THE GENTILES

Peter's vision concerns clean and unclean animals with a command to kill and eat.

> He saw heaven opened and something like a large sheet being let down to earth by its four corners. It contained all kinds of four-footed animals, as well as reptiles of the earth and birds of the air. Then a voice told him, 'Get up, Peter. Kill and eat.' 'Surely not, Lord!', Peter replied. 'I have never eaten anything impure or unclean.'

---

[22] France, *Matthew*, 234.

[23] Jeremias Joachim, *Jesus' Promise to the Nations* (London: SCM, 1966), 73.

[24] F.F. Bruce, *The Book of the Acts*, New International Commentary on the New Testament (Grand Rapids, MI: Eerdmans, 1975), 39.

The voice spoke to him a second time, 'Do not call anything impure that God has made clean' (Acts 10:10-15).

Then he heard the Spirit direct him to Cornelius. By the help of the Holy Spirit, Cornelius and Peter discovered the purpose of the vision. Peter concluded from his vision that he must not call anyone common or unclean. The vision not only revealed how he must act toward Gentiles but also God's acceptance of the Gentiles (Acts 10:34).

When Peter engaged in an itinerant ministry visiting the scattered Christian communities of Judea, he reached Lydda (Acts 9:32-35). There he healed a paralytic man named Aeneas. In Joppa he raised a dead woman named Tabitha (Acts 9:36-41). The significance of these healings is found in the fact that the news spread throughout the locale and beyond. Most likely the population was semi-Gentile.[25]

Peter learned that God does not favor one nation over another (Acts 10:34-35), but anyone and/or any nation who fears him and acts rightly, is acceptable to him.

3.3.2 BARNABAS' WILLINGNESS FOR THE GENTILES

Barnabas had the gift of encouragement and faith. He felt deep compassion for souls and was committed to ministry among the Gentiles of Antioch (Acts 11:22-23). His heart was filled with joy and excitement because of the fact that the gospel was not only preached to Israel but also to the Gentiles and many who heard the gospel received the Lord (Acts 11:24). Barnabas also urged new believers to evangelize others vigorously in spite of obstacles.[26] Therefore, the Antiochenes honored the word of the Lord and received eternal life.

Presenting Jesus Christ as Messiah to people who knew nothing of the hope of Israel could be meaningless. But the Greek terms *kurios*, 'lord,' and *soter*, 'savior,' were widely known to the religious world of the eastern Mediterranean. In fact, many were trying to find a lord and savior in various mystery cults.[27] After their conversion, people in Antioch came to realize that all their religious efforts were futile. Now they had found a shelter for their souls in Christ who is the God of every creature. They further maintained their evangelistic enthusiasm to serve the Lord and eventually became witnesses for the Lord.

3.3.3 RESPONSE OF THE GENTILES TO THE GOSPEL

The power of Holy Spirit was marvelously manifested among the Gentiles. The descent of the Spirit on the Gentiles who gathered in Cornelius' house was much the same as it had been when the disciples

---

[25] Bruce, *The Book of the Acts*, 39.

[26] Bruce, *The Book of the Acts*, 227.

[27] Bruce, *The Book of the Acts*, 225.

received the Spirit at Pentecost. They spoke in tongues and proclaimed the mighty work of God (Acts 10:45-46). In 1 Corinthians 12:13 Paul wrote, 'In one Spirit we were all baptized into one body, whether Jews or Greeks.'

Having received the good news and the power of the Holy Spirit, their hearts were filled with joy and enthusiasm; and Barnabas and Paul encouraged the Gentile converts to continue in the grace of God (Acts 13:43):

> On the next Sabbath almost the whole city gathered to hear the word of the Lord. When the Jews saw the crowds, they were filled with jealousy and talked abusively against what Paul was saying (Acts 13:44).

A great crowd of the Gentiles visited the synagogue and sat down. They were eager to listen to the message, which the Jews found unacceptable. The Jewish leaders had hard hearts and became very irritated with the preaching of Paul.[28]

Paul and Barnabas, seeing the jealousy of the Jews, began to preach clearly that it was right and proper for the Jews to hear the good news first. However, the Jews refused. This opened the way to the Gentiles (Acts 13:46). To justify their ministry among the Gentiles, Paul and Barnabas cited the scriptures from Isaiah: 'I have made you a light for the Gentiles that you may bring salvation to the ends of the earth' (Is. 49:6). This eventually became a pattern for Paul's evangelistic ministry (Rom. 11:11) followed in city after city, even in Rome (Acts 28:25-28).

The Gentile Christians who put their faith in Christ joyfully extolled the goodness of God (13:48). They were not only the recipients of the good news and the baptism of the Holy Spirit, but also yielded their allegiance to Jesus as Lord.[29] They took the message of God and spread it to the areas surrounding Antioch. This was entirely new in foreign lands (Acts 13:49). The irony is that these people were 'Gentiles' yet they were included in the privilege of knowing the gospel as chosen people, while the chosen nation of Israel excluded themselves by their unbelief.[30]

It is obvious that Israel was the light to the world and this command came from God. The mission of the Messiah was/is not confined to Israel but goes beyond prejudiced racial boundaries to bring salvation 'to the ends of the earth' (Is. 49:6). Jesus gave the same commission to the disciples before ascending to heaven:

---

[28] Everett F. Harrison, *Acts: The Expanding Church* (Chicago, IL: Moody, 1973), 216.

[29] Bruce, *The Book of the Acts*, 225-26.

[30] Harrison, *Acts*, 217.

You will receive power when the Holy Spirit comes on you and you will be my witnesses in Jerusalem, and in all Judea and Samaria, and to the ends of the earth (Acts 1:8).

Jesus himself affirmed that the living word of God should be known to the ends of the earth. Those who have been saved by the blood of Jesus must preach the gospel of salvation. Jesus demonstrated his mission to the Gentiles through his ministry among them and through the powerful statement cited above.

IV. Conclusion

In the study of these passages, several significant points have emerged regarding the concept of light. First of all, to be the light characterizes our life and life's goal. It is a life of sacrifice and mission for others. God has chosen the Israelites for a particular purpose: to be the light to the world (Is. 49:6). Their mission is to make God's name known to the Gentiles. The book of Isaiah particularly reveals that our lives are extraordinarily ordained for a specific purpose—to be the light to the world.

Through the study of the mission of Jesus, it has been observed that his compassion and divine power were not restricted to a group of people but open to anyone who came to him for help. His mercy and love are not limited nor is his commission bound to his own people. In fact, he held special compassion toward the Gentiles who needed to hear the good news of salvation.

This wider scope of Jesus' mission is reflected in his strategy and attitude, and this should be part of our missions strategy and attitude. The natural human tendency is to concentrate on a familiar level of work instead of broadening or expanding to other dimensions. The church sometimes makes boundaries with its own rules that will eventually limit its scope and perspective. This will never bring the full meaning of being light. Love and compassion for souls are the essential elements as one endeavors to fulfill the call.

Without the significant contribution of the disciples in their preaching of the gospel to the Gentiles, the good news of Christ would never have spread to the world. It is their revolutionary awareness of God's purpose for the Gentiles that made the first-century 'world evangelization' possible. God mobilized human resources as a means of fulfilling his purpose. God mobilized human power. The power of Holy Spirit was evident in their ministry to the Gentiles as they shone as the light of Christ.

Likewise, as the light of the world, we must take up this challenge. Sensitivity to the spiritual agony of people and commitment to preach the gospel to the lost should be the work of every servant of God.

Thousands in the world are in darkness and many places have no viable Christian witness. This truth should serve to remind Asian Christians of the urgent and primary calling of the church. Pastors who are uncertain of this primary call need to receive a fresh challenge from the word of God. The church as the body of Christ is called to shine with the living gospel. Those who are sent across cultural boundaries as missionaries need to renew their burden and love for their dying souls instead of settling for the contentment of routine. The effect of the light is penetrating and it quickly chases away darkness and makes every place bright with hope and joy. But, if we fail to be the light, the Lord's challenge to the exiled Israel could be ours.

Chosen Israel, called forth as the servant of Yahweh, neglected its call. But the moment of awakening came in the midst of suffering. God reiterated specifically the role of the servant of God (Is. 42:1-4). God compelled them to be the light and witness to the world as part of his plan. Yahweh promised them restoration and deliverance from the bondage of Babylon. The churches, more often than not, make the same mistake. We need to be constantly reminded of the ultimate call by diligently studying the word of God. This will help to bring us back to the very place we were called and commissioned.

Many tribal communities in the deep mountains of northern Luzon in the Philippines, for instance, have never heard the gospel nor known the existence of the supreme God. This reality of darkness and the call for the church to be the light and thus bring the light to darkened humanity should compel God's people to take the call seriously. Undoubtedly, it should be the call of the church to reach every tribe and every city that desperately needs to hear the living word of God. The call to bring the light from God and to become the light itself is a noble mission. Jesus Christ is the example. Bringing the light to the people who walk in darkness (Is. 9:2) is a rewarding undertaking in spite of difficulties.

The *Missio Dei*, the mission of God, requires that for God's redemptive purpose for the nations to be fulfilled, all believers need to respond to God's call to his mission. As God himself started this mission, Jesus Christ pursued it through his life, death, and resurrection. The disciples reached the Gentiles, which often meant their deaths, and today the church is called to fulfill the same mission. In a narrower sense, individual believers are to be the light of the world in the streets, the nearby villages, to pagan worshippers, to those in prison. We must undertake the redemptive work initiated by God. On the other hand, the church of Jesus Christ as a collective entity is called to unity around the lordship of Jesus to being his light to the lost world.

CHAPTER 3

Gentiles Who Associated with the People of God

There are numerous examples of a close relationship between the Israelites and the Gentiles. Several became part of the lineage of Abraham. This demonstrates God's embracing position and unlimited love toward those who are non-Jewish. It also indicates God's intention of using them to fulfill his plan and purpose. Through the discussion of this subject, God's openness toward the Gentiles is clearly seen.

I. The Old Testament

1.1 Melchizedek

Genesis 14:18-23 depicts an interesting interaction between Melchizedek and Abraham. Verse 18 notes Melchizedek's welcome of Abraham as he returned from his victory over Kedorlaomer. Melchizedek brought out bread and wine and blessed Abraham in the name of God Most High, maker of heaven and earth. Such a gesture indicates gratitude to Abraham, who had won the battle for peace, freedom and prosperity.[1] Melchizedek was the first priest named in Scripture and was a priest-king over Salem (Jerusalem). He was a Gentile who openly confessed his faith in Yahweh.[2] Melchizedek was recognized by Abraham as a member of the divine priesthood when he gave him one tenth of the entire booty taken from the enemy. This was according to the general custom of giving the tenth to God.[3]

The use of the term 'God Most High' is open to dispute. The term was used to refer both to Yahweh (vv. 18-19) and the god of the Phoenicians and Canaanites.[4] According to Phoenician theology by Philo Herennius of Byblos, the deity Eliun ('most high' or *hypsistos* in Greek) appeared

---

[1] C.F. Keil and F. Delitzsch, *The Pentateuch*, Commentary on the Old Testament, vol. 1, trans. James Martin (Grand Rapids, MI: Eerdmans, 1978), 207.

[2] Walter C. Kaiser, Jr., 'Israel's Missionary Call', in Ralph D. Winter and Steven C. Hawthorne (eds), *Perspectives on the World Christian Movement* (Pasadena, CA: William Carey Library, 1992), 25.

[3] Kaiser, 'Israel's Missionary Call', 25.

[4] Glasser, *Kingdom and Mission*, 61.

as the oldest god.[5] Melchizedek, as a Gentile priest and definitely not from the Abrahamic line, was referred to as the priest of 'God Most High' (Heb. 7:1). This mysterious reality yields no clues in the search to find adequate answers. The more mysterious fact is that there is no account of his descent, or his birth and death. He stands forth in the Scriptures, 'without father or without mother, without genealogy, without beginning of days or end of life' (7:3).

Therefore, Melchizedek is pictured in a variety ways: 1) he is a type of a celestial being or an angel; 2) he is like one of the ancient patriarchs; 3) he is viewed as the Rabbi and church father; 4) he is an onlooker near the beginning of the revelation of God; and 5) he came into the light of history from the darkness of paganism. This manifestation reveals a priesthood of universal implications, which existed at the origin of the world, and will one day be restored again. In these respects, 'this king of Salem and the priest of the "Most High" God was a type of the God-King and eternal High Priest, Jesus Christ.'[6]

Melchizedek represents a non-Abrahamic tradition enlightened by the revelation of God. He belongs to the nations outside that of Abraham.[7] He is the first person with whom Abraham closely associated in terms of receiving and giving divine blessing. It is an amazing fact to grasp that God permitted the Gentile priest to bless the chosen man of God. It is also surprising that Abraham received his blessing with food that was offered. Out of this account, a few missiological points can be made. First of all, this perspective notes God's inclusive attitude and unrestricted heart toward the Gentiles. It demonstrates that God can employ a non-believing person to fulfill his divine will. Secondly, it denotes the position of God's people in dealing with unbelievers. Christians unnecessarily tend to make a boundary under a declaration of safety. Many Christians feel fear when engaging in conversation with people outside the church. Such attitudes indicate a negative analogy when light does not exert itself to remove darkness but that light seems to be kept within a comfort or safety zone. How then does light accomplish its role?

Thirdly, this story gives us a lesson of the importance of developing a sense of openness. Openness does not mean freedom to follow what the world teaches. It does not mean freedom to conform to a worldly life. It means an intention to approach people to bring them to feast at the King's table. This openness should extend to a dialogue with diverse Christian groups, breaking through denominational boundaries. It must also be applied in the context of other religious groups of people in a

---

[5] John E. Alsup, 'Typology', *The Anchor Bible Dictionary*, vol. 6, ed. D.N, Freedman (New York: Doubleday, 1992), 684.

[6] Keil and Delitzsch, *The Pentateuch*, 208-209.

[7] Roger E. Hedlund, *Mission to Man in the Bible* (Madras: Evangelical Literature Service, 1985), 86.

manner that is not hurtful if we believe they have a right to hear the good news of Jesus Christ. Often Christian church leaders have negative mindsets as if they have compromised the gospel. A fact we have to grasp is that God is God of the universe. Christ died for all sinners and governs, not only in the church and Christian life, but also over all people he has created. The only difference is that the ones who have received the gospel recognize God's rule in their lives while others may not be aware of such an important fact. Therefore, our task is to invite them into the Kingdom of God, under the lordship of Jesus. Although it is understood that Satan rules in the lives of people who have not received the message of the gospel yet, if we acknowledge God's reign over all the cosmos, both seen and unseen, ultimately God rules over all organic beings, including Satan.

Melchizedek's account is a window of opportunity to discover some significant missiological implications, which we can apply in our work for God.

1.2 Tamar

Genesis 38 notes an interesting episode that took place between Judah and Tamar. A sexual relationship occurred between the father-in-law and the daughter-in-law. It does not just end there but is significant because Tamar, the Gentile woman, was privileged to be included in the genealogy of the Messiah. The Scripture shows that Tamar was a Canaanite and Judah's three sons were married to her. It was indicated that God's people, who had been settlers in Adullam in the hill country southwest of Jerusalem, tended to mix with the local Canaanites. Judah's wife was a Canaanite.[8] Judah was unsuccessful because he lost his two sons. The Scriptures do not elaborate on the nature of Er's sin. Verse 6 simply says, 'Judah got a wife for Er, his first son, and her name was Tamar. But Er, Judah's firstborn, was wicked in the Lord's sight; so the Lord put him to death.' According to levirate practice, when the firstborn son dies, the second son should take the wife of his older brother.[9] Thus, Onan was responsible to undertake for her, then came Shelah, the youngest son (vv. 8 and 11).

The story continues and after God struck Onan, Tamar had to wait until Shelah grew up before she could take him as her husband. But she disguised herself as a prostitute and appeared before Judah, her father-in-law who thought she was a sacred prostitute. Pagan worship of the goddess of fertility was observed among the Canaanites and condemned by the prophets (cf. Hos. 4:14). Why did Tamar do that? Tamar had no

---

[8] Roland E. Murphy, *Genesis*, Jerome Biblical Commentary (Englewood Cliffs, NY: Prentice, Hall, 1968), 39.

[9] Murphy, *Genesis*, 39.

motivation of lust or religious obligation; she only craved offspring. However, Tamar's behavior was considered adultery since she was the legal wife of Shelah. Thus, Judah was responsible for executing the penalty of stoning her (cf. Deut. 22:22-24).[10] He was guilty because he was driven by lust while Tamar was moved by her earnest desire for children.

God was gracious to Judah who humbly confessed his sin. God's blessing was upon his offspring born through sin. This episode explains the predominance of the Perez clan, from which David was descended and Jesus Christ was born. The Gentile woman, Tamar, became an ancestor of Jesus and was the first Gentile woman to join the Abrahamic line. It reminds us that the limited minds of human beings can never understand the hidden will of God for each individual. This incident also demonstrates God's paramount grace, which expands beyond our common ability to comprehend. God's embrace and acceptance of the Gentiles are accentuated in this story.

1.3 Jethro, Moses' Father-in-Law

In Exodus 18:8-10 Moses recalled Yahweh's accomplishments on their behalf and his dealings with Pharaoh. He reviewed the difficult obstacles they met along the way. Highlighted are God's protection and salvation in each moment. Moses' story was about how Yahweh shielded Israel by his power.

Jethro was a priest of Midian (Ex. 18:1) and the Bible does not give much information about him. Chapter 18 presents Jethro's vital role and presence in Moses' life. Moses' openness and dependence on Jethro reveal how much he trusted him. In fact, twice he told Jethro the story about Egypt's defeat and God's victory (vv. 1, 8). Cassuto says, 'A repetition of Moses' confession is a kind of mirror-image of the declaration of the proof of Yahweh's Presence.'[11] Verses 9-12 indicate Jethro's joyous response. He was delighted to hear about all the good things the Lord had done for Israel in rescuing them from the hand of the Egyptians. Jethro said, 'Praise be to the Lord, who rescued you from the hand of the Egyptians and of Pharaoh, and who rescued the people from the hand of the Egyptians. Now I know that the Lord is greater than all other gods, for he did this to those who had treated Israel arrogantly.' Then Jethro, Moses' father-in-law, brought burnt offerings and other sacrifices to God, and Aaron came with all the elders of Israel to eat bread with Jethro in the presence of God.

---

[10] Murphy, *Genesis*, 39.
[11] U. Cassuto, *A Commentary on the Book of Exodus* (Jerusalem: Magnes, 1987), 216.

His expression (v. 10), 'Praise be to the Lord', is interpreted not as a prayer but as a kerygmatic utterance intended 'to express joy in God's gracious acts and to proclaim those acts to the world.'[12] He makes a significant point in verse 11 when he proclaims his faith through his own experience. The victories that Moses shared with him, together with what he was already familiar with, directed him to conclude; 'now I know' that 'Yahweh is greater than all gods.' This statement implies that Jethro believes what he has already suspected that Yahweh is, indeed, the God among gods. He confesses that Yahweh is greater than any other gods. In a sense, he confirms to himself what he believes was right.[13]

Jethro sacrificed a burnt offering (v. 12), which was considered an act of his faith. He then took part in a communion meal that included Aaron and the elders of Israel.[14] The elders represent the entire people of Israel.[15] Jethro, the Gentile priest, made the confession that the God of Israel was almighty. Jethro's association with them was built through offering the sacrifice. This gesture surprisingly enabled the Israelites to recognize his priestly function and role.

This scene demonstrates that in times of desperate need, God can cause any Gentile to become an instrument of assistance to his people and cause him or her to become a part of fulfilling his plan. It can also be seen that God has unique ways of employing anyone for the completion of his work.

1.4 Hobab, Jethro's Son

In Numbers 10:29-34 notice that Hobab is the son of Moses' father-in-law (Ex. 2:18). They are brothers-in-law. The Israelites are camped at the sacred mountain, the 'mountain of Yahweh.'[16] The reference from Judges 4:11 supports the fact that the descendants of Hobab dwelt among the tribes of Israel.

Verse 29 notes that Moses asked Hobab the Midianite to lead the Israelites into a wilderness that was unfamiliar to the people. He told Hobab that he needed someone who had experience and could guide them through the wilderness. He refused Moses' request but desired to return to his own country. Moses urged him to help.

---

[12] W.S. Towner, '"Blessed Be YHWH" and "Blessed Art Thou, YHWH": The Modulation of a Biblical Formula', *Catholic Biblical Quarterly* 30 (1968), 387, 389.

[13] John I. Durham, *Exodus*, Word Biblical Commentary 3 (Waco, TX: Word, 1987), 244.

[14] Durham, *Exodus*, 244.

[15] Durham, *Exodus*, 245.

[16] Martin Noth, *Numbers: A Commentary* (Philadelphia, PA: Westminster, 1968), 79.

Hobab could have helped Israel in several ways: as their eyes to evaluate the countryside or as an elder to give counsel[17] and as one who certainly knew the places to camp. Perhaps Hobab had the same understanding of God as Jethro and the same impression of a living God who performed signs and wonders, who is all-powerful and almighty (Ex. 11:8-10).

As a reward, Moses promised Hobab to share 'whatever good things the Lord gives us' (Nu. 10:32). In the present context, a reward or a gift could only be land.[18] After his first rejection of Moses' offer (v. 30), Hobab then agreed to go with them. He had an interesting experience while they were looking for a resting place. Verses 33-34 states,

> So they set out from the mountain of the LORD and traveled for three days. The Ark of the Covenant of the LORD went before them during those three days to find them a place to rest. The cloud of the LORD was over them by day when they set out from the camp.

An intriguing fact is that Moses chose a leader not from among his own people but on the basis of his previous experience with Hobab. Here, Moses' recognition of the leadership ability of a Gentile revealed that he was not antagonistic toward Gentiles and there was no pride of ethnicity as the chosen people. On the other hand, Hobab's sincere work for the Israelites, rather than for his own people, was highly recognized. The signs and wonders performed by God among his people, eye-witnessed by Hobab, would be important to increase his faith. They further increased his desire to serve the Israelites. This case illustrates once more the close involvement and relationship of a Gentile with God's chosen people.

1.5 Rahab

Joshua 2 recounts the conquest of Canaan and imbedded within the victory is a Gentile woman, Rahab, whose help was essential. She was a prostitute in Jericho. Prostitution has often been connected to 'Canaanite' fertility cults and Rahab may have been a priestess and sacred prostitute.[19] The role that she played had nothing to do with her profession. The two spies sent by Joshua from Shittim happened to enter into Rahab's house (vv. 1-2). Aiding the two spies was originally seen as a betrayal of the

---

[17] B. Maarsingh, *Numbers: A Practical Commentary*, trans. John Vriend (Grand Rapids, MI: Eerdmans, 1985), 37.

[18] Maarsingh, *Numbers*, 78-79.

[19] Alberto Soggin, *Joshua: A Commentary* (Philadelphia, PA: Westminster, 1972), 39.

city.[20] The bold action of Rahab could even have led to her death. This Gentile woman's courageous action facilitated the Israelites' conquest of Jericho.

According to *The Bible and Recent Archaeology,* Jericho is a '70-foot high Tell es-Sultan, six miles north of the Dead Sea.'[21] The walls of the city that date from the Early Bronze Age reveal that a community existed there between 2900-2300 BC. The walls of the Middle Bronze Age indicate a series of building stages. The last level is apparent because of a new kind of wall fortification defense-scheme.[22]

Verses 3 and 4 explain that the king of Jericho sent messengers to tell Rahab to bring out the men who had entered her house but she took and hid them. It was an act of faith. Verses 8-11 reveal more of her faith. She was assured of what Yahweh, God of Israel, had done. It records,

> Before the spies lay down for the night, she went up on the roof and said to them, 'I know that the Lord has given this land to you and that a great fear of you has fallen on us, so that all who live in this country are melting in fear because of you. We have heard how the Lord dried up the water of the Red Sea for you when you came out of Egypt, and what you did to Sihon and Og, the two kings of the Amorites east of the Jordan, whom you completely destroyed. When we heard of it, our hearts melted and everyone's courage failed because of you, for the Lord your God is God in heaven above and on the earth below.'

Rahab requested that she be given 'a sure sign' to spare the lives of her household (v. 12) when the Israelites returned to conquer. The men told her to tie a scarlet cord in the window (through which she later let them down, v. 17), then the lives of her family would be saved. Her strong trust and faith eventually played a key role in the salvation of her entire household.

The New Testament refers in several instances to Rahab as an example of faith. She is one of three women with remarkable reputations who are integrated into the genealogy of the Messiah (Mt. 1:5-6). She is known as a woman of faith (Heb. 11:31). James 2:25 recognizes Rahab along with Abraham. These examples underscore the role and importance of Rahab in the narrative. Indeed, her strong faith is an outstanding example not only for the Israelites, but also for the people of God today.

---

[20] Murphy, *Genesis*, 126.

[21] Dame K. Kenyon, *The Bible and Recent Archaeology* (Atlanta, GA: John Knox, 1978), 36-40.

[22] Trent C. Butler, *Joshua*, Word Biblical Commentary 7 (Waco, TX: Word, 1983), 32.

1.6 Ruth

Ruth is another Gentile woman who became a descendant of Abraham. Ruth's story perhaps closely parallels that of Tamar. She was a Moabite who was unusual because she was determined to make something of her life. Her mother-in-law Naomi's husband, Elimelech, died and unfortunately Ruth's husband Mahlon also died leaving no child. She became a young widow (Ru. 1:5). Chapter 2 notes the tension of Ruth's status as an alien. As Naomi's daughter-in-law, living as a stranger within a Hebrew context, she must have encountered difficulties being accepted by Naomi's people.[23] More difficult may have been the continuous travel between Bethlehem and other locations. She went from Bethlehem to Moab and back to Bethlehem; then to the field and back to Bethlehem; to the threshing floor returning again to Bethlehem; to the town gate, and finally settled in Bethlehem 'the house of bread.'[24] Although she met difficult times as a Gentile and frequently traveled in addition to suffering the hardships of simple survival, Ruth accompanied Naomi faithfully. This reflects her sincere and caring heart for her mother-in-law. Ruth, in fact, was the breadwinner in the family.

Verse 2 narrates the conversation between the two women. Ruth approached her mother-in-law for permission to glean grain in the field. Here, 'Let me go' (v. 2) expresses two different meanings: 'firm resolve'[25] and a 'polite request.'[26] Ruth perhaps retains a polite manner and yet was decisive in her plan to go. The Mosaic law called for particular care for the alien, the orphan, and the widow in that harvesters intentionally allowed some of the grain in their fields to remain for the poor and indigent (Lev. 19:9-10; 23:22; Deut. 24:19).

Chapter 4 depicts the marriage of Boaz and Ruth, which is one of the highlights of the book of Ruth. This eventually led Ruth into the lineage of Jesus. The laws of marriage were different in those days (Deut. 25). One law stated that distant relatives were under obligation to marry someone in Ruth's position. However, the kinsman-redeemer, Boaz, was under no obligation to contract a levirate marriage with her. Naomi, in fact, pled with Ruth to find a marriage partner in her own country instead of staying with her in such poor living circumstances. Neither of them had a legal right to compel marriage with any of Elimelech's relatives.[27] However, one observation may be that Boaz was uncertain whether Ruth

---

[23] Daniel I. Block, *Judges, Ruth*, New American Commentary (Nashville, TN: Broadman & Holman, 1999), 650.

[24] Block, *Judges, Ruth*, 650.

[25] Thomas O. Lambdin, *Introduction to Biblical Hebrew* (New York: Scribners, 1971), 170-71.

[26] Block, *Judges, Ruth*, 652.

[27] Kirsten Nielsen, *Ruth* (Louisville, KY: Westminster/John Knox, 1997), 85.

compromised him while he was asleep. Boaz's decision to act unconventionally is rather to save his own honor.[28] Nonetheless, after their marriage Ruth gave birth to a son, Obed, which means, 'One who serves' (v. 17). He became the father of Jesse, who became the father of David. A motif of some weight in the book of Ruth is loyalty to the family with corresponding fertility, as well as Ruth's faithfulness to her mother-in-law. Such faithfulness directs her into the genealogy of Christ.

1.7 Bathsheba

2 Samuel 11:1-27 relates the story of David's affair with Bathsheba (vv. 2-5). She was the wife of Uriah the Hittite. She appears as a passive figure in this account, which is different from Rahab, who made a visible contribution through her bold act. Bathsheba's case is also distinct from that of Tamar, whose act is justifiable in terms of wanting offspring. However, Bathsheba was simply summoned to come to the king, and he had his way with her. One finds no way of discovering Bathsheba's feelings. She may have been aware of the peril wherein adultery was directing her. Or this incident may have caused her to feel honor at having fascinated the king.[29] No matter the prime cause, Bathsheba entered the genealogy of Christ.

Bathsheba's husband was in battle with the Ammonites when the unpleasant episode took place. Bathsheba's beauty attracted David to the point he initiated the adultery which caused her pregnancy. Verses 6-13 disclose how the king conspired against this loyal and upright man. David called Uriah, who was still in the battle, to come home and rest. But Uriah never returned home but stayed at the royal palace and slept at the entrance with others. It has been said that 'Uriah drunk is more pious than David sober!'[30] Uriah is a good Yahwistic name, meaning 'Yahweh is my light.' This implies that he was born and grew up in Israel.[31] As the meaning of his name stands, although not an Israelite, he followed Yahweh's way and teaching. Uriah's expression in verse 11 is remarkable as he uttered, 'The ark and Israel and Judah are standing in tents, and my master Joab and my lord's men are camped in the open fields. How could I go to my house to eat and drink and lie with my wife? As surely as you live, I will not do such a thing.'

---

[28] Danna Fewell and David Gunn, *Compromising Redemption: Relating Characters in the Book of Ruth* (Louisville, KY: John Knox Press, 1990), 86-93.

[29] Hans Wilhelm Hertzberg, *1 and 2 Samuel: A Commentary*, trans. J.S. Bowden (Philadelphia, PA: Westminster, 1964), 310.

[30] P.R. Ackroyd, *The Second Book of Samuel*, Cambridge Bible Commentary (Cambridge: Cambridge University Press, 1977), 102.

[31] A.A. Anderson, *2 Samuel*, Word Biblical Commentary 11 (Dallas TX: Word, 1989), 153.

When his wicked device did not work, David assigned him, through Joab, to a sector which was manned by Ammonite 'crack troops.' Joab had to coax Uriah's death in battle. This method proved to be the best solution.[32] David then brought Bathsheba to his palace as he had in an earlier incident with Abigail.[33] Then, the son was born but the child was not named.

However, the account of David does not end here. He experiences a considerable amount of judgment and condemnation by God. In chapter 12, the prophet Nathan presents a parable to the king that is defined as a 'juridical parable', one that pretends an actual-life violation of the regulation in the form of a parable shared with the guilty in order to direct him to make a verdict upon himself.[34] With his realization of sin, David confessed to Nathan (v. 13). He further repented by way of fasting and acknowledging God's justice at the same time. However, on the seventh day he lost his child (v. 18). He was struck by God.

Verse 24 notes that Bathsheba later bore a son named Solomon whom God loved. The death of the unlawful child was interpreted as a divine penalty for David's illegal relationship with Bathsheba. Only the birth of Solomon could be considered as a sign of divine pardon.[35] Solomon was affirmed as heir and confirmed as the successor. Thus, Bathsheba, the Gentile woman, became an ascendant of the Messiah, Jesus Christ.

1.8 Naaman

2 Kings 5 depicts the healing of Naaman who was a chief officer of the army of the king of Aram. He was a rare Gentile in terms of experiencing the power of the God of the Israelites. The account starts with Elisha's cure of Naaman's leprosy. In fact, the story is referred to as a 'power demonstration narrative.'[36] A 'leper' may suffer from various forms of leprosy. In Naaman's case, it was a skin disease that became white, perhaps a dryness of the skin tissue (v. 27). It is not what modern medicine understands leprosy to be.[37] Obviously, his disease was such that he was not forced to dwell in a separate place.

A young girl's assuring words about Elisha hinted that he should find the prophet. It is astonishing that a person like Naaman believed a maiden of Samaria. 'He would cure him of his leprosy' (v. 3) implies that the

---

[32] Anderson, *2 Samuel*, 155.

[33] Hertzberg, *1 and 2 Samuel*, 312.

[34] Anderson, *2 Samuel*, 160.

[35] Anderson, *2 Samuel*, 165.

[36] S.J. deVries, *Prophet against Prophet* (Waco, TX: Word, 1985), 54, 57, 118.

[37] T.R. Hobbs, *2 Kings*, Word Biblical Commentary 13 (Waco TX: Word, 1985), 13, 63.

reknown of Elisha as a miracle worker was widespread.[38] Naaman clearly had a strong desire to be healed. He even took gifts with him to offer Elisha when he left for Samaria.

Much to his disappointment Elisha merely commanded that Naaman wash in the Jordan. Verse 10 says, 'Go, wash yourself seven times in the Jordan, and your flesh will be restored and you will be cleansed.' Ritual cleansing was commonly practiced in the Ancient Near East. The origin of ritual purification and cleansing in rivers can be traced to the primal veneration of river gods in the Ancient Near East. However, none of the Semitic gods of healing are connected with water. Even if the association could be made, there is little similarity to Naaman's situation. Water is a mark of cleansing in the Old Testament and in the Ancient Near East.[39]

This wealthy and powerful man was simply instructed to wash himself for healing. Dipping his body in the Jordan to fulfill his goal was a humiliating act for Naaman. The request infuriated him. The greatness of the gift that he brought faded in comparison. Perhaps, in his mind, there was some better means to a cure. However, Naaman listened to his attendant's advice and stepped down into the water and dipped himself seven times. It was truly a way of indicating his humility. His flesh was restored like that of a little child and he was cleansed completely (v. 14). This divine experience absolutely changed his perception of Yahweh, God of Israel. Verse 15 well notes Naaman's confession, 'Now I know that there is no God in the entire world except in Israel'. Naaman came to understand that healing would take place only in Israel, and through Israel's God. This was an admission that the Gentile, Naaman, had found a new faith in God. It is a significant testimony because the Gentiles then realized that God's power would expand beyond Israel's jurisdiction and particular ethnicity. This proves that he is the universal God who demonstrates his work and power even among non-believers.

II. The New Testament

2.1 The Ethiopian Eunuch

Acts 8:26-31 describes the conversion of the Ethiopian eunuch through Philip. Philip courageously preached the gospel to the Samaritans. As generally understood, there was an unfriendly relationship between Judea and Samaria. Historically, these two people groups were divided. According to the Fourth Gospel, both John the Baptist and Jesus had spent quite a while in this area (Jn. 3:23; 4:4-42); their ministry could have provided a base on which Philip was able to get access.[40]

---

[38] Hobbs, *2 Kings*, 64.

[39] Hobbs, *2 Kings*, 65.

[40] Bruce, *Acts*, 165.

Verses 26-40 provide an interesting account of Philip's meeting with the Ethiopian eunuch on the road. Greeks and Romans were exceptionally enthralled with dark-skinned Africans. Along the way Philip encountered an Ethiopian eunuch. The eunuch was 'an important official in charge of all the treasure of Candace, queen of the Ethiopians' (v. 27). He had gone to Jerusalem to worship, and on the way home he was reading the Scriptures from Isaiah, sitting in his chariot (vv. 27-28). God's direction of Philip's encounter with the Ethiopian would have been just as intriguing to 'first-century Romans or Greeks', because, from their perspective, Ethiopians lived at the southern rim of the earth (Acts 1:8).[41]

God sought to fulfill his purpose which offered the scope of the church's mission (Lk. 24:47; Acts 1:8). If the gospel reached an Ethiopian soon after its beginning, it was clearly assumed that the good news would be shared among all the nations. The commission from Jesus (Acts 1:8) set out not only the task of preaching but also gave guidance regarding the geographical aspects of the expansion: Jerusalem (Acts 6:8–8:3), Judea and Samaria (Acts 8:4-25) and to the ends of the earth (Acts 8:26-40). It also predicted the fullness of the mission to the Gentiles to come (chs. 13–28).

The author of Acts does not identify the eunuch as either a proselyte, a Gentile convert to Judaism, or a God-fearing Gentile believer of Jewish monotheism. Luke presented him only as a devout follower of the Jewish faith.[42] Philip approached the chariot to engage in conversation under the direction of the Spirit (Acts 8:29). Although the eunuch read the Scriptures, he could not understand them. It certainly spoke of needing someone's help in interpreting the Scriptures. Philip expounded Isaiah 53 and explained the fulfilment of the Scriptures in Jesus' life, death and victorious resurrection and exaltation. The eunuch was excited in hearing about Jesus. This led him to be baptized in the water.

Acts 8:36-38 reads:

As they traveled along the road, they came to some water and the eunuch said, 'Look, here is water. Why shouldn't I be baptized?' And he gave orders to stop the chariot. Then both Philip and the eunuch went down into the water and Philip baptized him.

After this event, the Spirit suddenly took Philip away and the eunuch went his way rejoicing. Here, joy is a sign of salvation, particularly of receiving the Holy Spirit (Acts 13:52).[43] 'The eunuch's conversion means the

---

[41] William J. Larkin, Jr., *Acts*, IVP New Testament Commentary (Downers Grove, IL: Inter-Varsity, 1995), 131.

[42] Larkin, *Acts*, 135.

[43] Larkin, *Acts*, 136.

inclusion of black Africans among the charter members of the faith...all of which symbolize from the beginning the African involvement in the new faith that spread throughout the world.'[44]

2.2 Cornelius

Cornelius is one of the outstanding Gentiles in the New Testament who was devoted to prayer, worship and the practice of the Jewish faith (Acts 10). He and his family were the first Gentiles who heard the gospel. As a centurion in the Roman army, he belonged to one of the outposts stationed in Judea.[45] During Jesus' earthly ministry, he met a Gentile centurion stationed in Capernaum who had a strong faith. Jesus said, 'I tell you the truth, I have not found anyone in Israel with such great faith. I say to you that many will come from the east and the west, and will take their places at the feast with Abraham, Isaac and Jacob in the kingdom of heaven' (Mt. 8:11). These predictions began to be accomplished through Cornelius.

Although Cornelius was a Gentile, he was a sincere worshipper of the God of Israel. These Gentiles were called 'God-fearers', which is not a technical term but one used for convenience.[46] If a Gentile was converted to Judaism, the requirement of circumcision was imposed. Therefore, they simply attended synagogue worship and followed the ethical principles of the Jewish life. Cornelius' regular prayer exercise and offering to help the poor appeared to be only a part of the Jewish religion.

F.F. Bruce comments on Acts 10:3-6: 'One afternoon at the regular time of prayer, a heavenly messenger appeared in a vision.... The angel's language is full of sacrificial terminology such as we find in the prescriptions for the Levitical offerings; Cornelius's acts of piety and charity had ascended into the divine presence like incense or the smoke of a sacrifice.'[47] God's acknowledgment of the 'memorial offering' (v. 4) of Cornelius was surprising. He was to send to a house in Joppa and invite Simon Peter, who was staying there, to come to visit him (vv. 5-6).

Interestingly, Peter saw a vision as he prayed while the men sent by Cornelius were on their way. Verses 11-13 state,

> He saw heaven opened and something like a large sheet being let down to earth by its four corners. It contained all kinds of four-footed animals, as well as reptiles of the earth and birds of the air. Then a voice told him 'Get up, Peter. Kill and eat.'

---

[44] C. Eric Lincoln, *Race, Religion and the Continuing American Dilemma* (New York: Hill and Wang, 1984), 24.

[45] Bruce, *Acts*, 201.

[46] Bruce, *Acts*, 203.

[47] Bruce, *Acts*, 203.

Peter protested against God's order by saying, 'I have never eaten anything impure or unclean' (v. 14). But God spoke the same words again and again. The voice of God overruled food restrictions. This vision implied that the work of God in bestowing the Spirit overruled the tradition which forbade involvement with Gentiles.[48] The large sheet from heaven and the voice both bore witness that all of God's creatures were now to be recognized as being clean and good and not to be rejected (Gen. 1:31; 1 Tim. 4:3).[49] While Peter was wondering about the implications of the vision, the Spirit spoke to him to accept the three men whom God would send to him (v. 20).

It was very obvious that God's plan for the salvation of Cornelius and his household was already set in place since the angel of God appeared to Cornelius. At the same time God spoke to Peter through a vision to accept the Gentiles.

In the meantime, Cornelius invited his relatives and friends to his home in anticipation of Peter's arrival. When Peter arrived, Cornelius paid him respect. Clearly the messenger of God was highly respected (vv. 25-26). While Peter was preaching, the Gentiles in Cornelius' house experienced the baptism of the Holy Spirit and people spoke in tongues and praised God (vv. 44-46). The Gentile Pentecost took place in Cornelius' home. Through this initial contact many more Gentiles were added into the salvation of Christ. The divine link between the chosen and the Gentile (clean and unclean) was established. Cornelius' case reveals the Spirit of God working outside the church. A sense of openness is required in our mission perspective.

III. Conclusion

This study particularly affirms God's openness to the Gentiles and their service to God's people in unique situations. It helps broaden our understanding of God's ways of interacting with all people. Several implications can be drawn from the above discussion, which may bring greater revelation of the universal God.

Firstly, one can immediately observe God's inclusion of the Gentiles. His election of the nation of Israel to fulfill his purpose did not mean that he severed his relationship with non-Israelites. He intended to include the Gentiles and invited them into relationship with himself. If it was necessary to use the Gentiles to implement his work, they were part of God's purposes. His sphere of ruler-ship was not limited to the Israelites but extended beyond them.

---

[48] Bruce, *Acts*, 217.
[49] Larkin, *Acts*, 158.

Secondly, God's salvation and healing power are intended for all human beings. His saving grace was never restricted to one nation. One example is reflected in the account of Naaman who was healed by the power of Yahweh, the God of Israel, whom Naaman never knew before. He merely acted in faith by obeying what Elisha commanded. Although it was humiliating to dip his body in the River Jordan, he did it. His obedience played a role in drawing God's saving grace upon him, and God extended his healing grace to a Gentile man.

Thirdly, faith and accountability are important elements in the Gentile's experience of divine blessing. Several of the above characters received faith to obey God's command. Hence, each took part in fulfilling God's divine will. Rahab is a prime example. Her commitment to implement the request of the two spies stands out although it was a risk to her own life.

Galatians 1:14 notes, 'He redeemed us in order that the blessing given to Abraham might come to the Gentiles through Christ Jesus, so that by faith we might receive the promise of the Spirit.' Galatians 3:18 supports this: 'For if the inheritance depends on the law, then it no longer depends on a promise, but God in his grace gave it to Abraham through a promise.' By faith and God's grace all of humanity is entitled to receive the privilege of the descendants of Abraham and enter into the sphere of the great blessing of salvation.

CHAPTER 4

Power in Mission

Scripture demonstrates that the manifestation of power is extremely significant in bringing the gospel to darkened minds, especially in the non-western world. Jesus' mission included many demonstrations of power as a means of proclaiming his Kingdom. Many would have not come to the Lord without seeing the concrete demonstration of God's power. Without doubt, it is one of the ways to lead people to faith. When Christ was ascending, he promised his disciples the Holy Spirit through whom they would receive power for mission. This seems to indicate that mission is impossible without power from above. The apostles followed the exact pattern of Jesus Christ. They performed miracles when they brought new lives into the Kingdom. If this is the pattern of Jesus, we, who are his followers in mission, ought to have the same power from the Holy Spirit.

Power encounter is found not only in the New Testament but also in the Old. One of the highlights in the demonstration of God's supernatural power in the Old Testament is Moses' confrontation with Pharaoh's magicians and sorcerers. Moses performed miracles before Pharaoh and the Egyptians. Walter Kaiser describes this incident as having an 'evangelistic thrust.'[1] God's intent was that the Egyptians would see I (Yahweh) am (Ex. 7:5; 9:14, 16; 12:38; 17:8, 22; 14:4, 18).

This chapter will discuss selected accounts of power manifestation from Scripture and supernatural occurrences from our experience among tribal people.[2] The power encounter has affected mission work greatly in my experience. Tribal people turned their hearts to Christ only through the experience of the power of God. Such events have literally served as an 'evangelistic thrust.' I believe that the discussion of practical miracle accounts bring heightened awareness of the importance of power manifestation in mission.

---

[1] Kaiser, *Mission in the Old Testament*, 21.
[2] The illustration comes from the Kankan-ey tribe of northern Luzon in the Philippines.

I. Miracle Records in the Old Testament

1.1 Divine Touch

One of the healing accounts in the Old Testament is drawn from Numbers 2 which reports Miriam's leprosy due to her rebellious attitude against Moses. God's three chosen leaders (Miriam, Aaron and Moses) had authority as priests or prophets. However, God imposed on Moses a distinctive and supreme authority.[3]

The complaint started with Moses' wife, the Cushite woman (Ethiopian) (e.g., Gen. 10:6) who was probably Moses' second wife.[4] The text does not say that Miriam and Aaron objected to Moses' leadership because of this woman (vv. 1-2). Aaron and Miriam claimed an equal status to Moses, with equal spiritual authority. The base for their objection and claim was erroneous (v. 2).[5]

The result of trying to usurp Moses' authority resulted in Miriam's leprosy. The term 'leprous' covers a wide range of skin diseases. Recorded as 'snow' in Numbers 5:2, it means a mild form of the disease (cf. Ex. 4:6). The comparison is its 'moistness', a reference to open wounds and ulcers.[6] However, Aaron and Miriam immediately admitted their foolishness and asked Moses to intercede with God for healing. Moses had immediate access to God, and spoke with him face to face. Miriam was healed through Moses' prayer and God's supernatural power. Although God punished Miriam by afflicting her with a miserable disease, his mercy was given in response to the intercession of Moses. The Lord's power healed Miriam.

The account of 2 Kings 20:1-11 contains Isaiah's two oracles—one regarding the sickness of Hezekiah, and the other his healing.[7] Hezekiah, the king of Judah, was so critically ill that he was even at the point of death, although the exact nature of his illness is not revealed. Several commentators believe that it was probably 'sore', which is related to a Hebrew root meaning, 'to be hot' and 'to be inflamed.' So, it is more or less a serious skin malady.[8] An oracle given to the king foretold his imminent death (v. 1). Upon hearing it, Hezekiah lifted up his voice to God. He faced the wall, which symbolizes his act of rejecting the world and turning to God alone.[9] His prayer was rather 'self-serving' and it

---

[3] Gordon J. Wenham, *Numbers: An Introduction and Commentary* (Downers Grove, IL: Inter-Varsity, 1981), 110.

[4] Wenham, *Numbers*, 111.

[5] Philip J. Budd, *Numbers*, Word Biblical Commentary 5 (Waco, TX: Word, 1984), 136.

[6] Budd, *Numbers*, 137.

[7] John Gray, *1 and 2 Kings* (London: SCM, 1970), 632.

[8] Hobbs, *2 Kings*, 291-92.

[9] Gray, *1 and 2 Kings*, 697.

reveals another image of the king.[10] It was a moment of intimate contact with God in a desperate situation. A prompt answer to his prayer came through Isaiah who declared that God would add fifteen years to Hezekiah's life. To grant the length of days is the only promise for honoring parents. This allusion is consistent with the Davidic theme running throughout, as in verse 4.[11] Yahweh healed Hezekiah and extended the reign of the king fifteen years more (v. 6). God's absolute power not only demonstrated healing but also the effect of lengthening human life.

1.2 God's Intervention in Battle

God's power was also revealed in war. Exodus 17:8-16 dramatically displays God's power extended during Israel's time of warfare. It was the first attack on Israel by the Amalekites who opposed the march of the Israelites after the miraculous passage through the Red Sea. The assault was insidious; an impious defiance of God.[12]

It was terrifying for the Israelites despite the deep impression and conviction that was left on them through their experience of manna (Ex. 16) and the water from the rock. Divine presence and help had, indeed, continuously been given them (17:1-7).

Moses' immediate reaction is found in 17:9: 'Moses said to Joshua, "Choose some of our men and go out to fight the Amalekites. Tomorrow I will stand on top of the hill with the staff of God in my hand."' Joshua commanded the forces of Israel, while Moses, Aaron, and Hur went up to the mountain to pray. Moses had the staff of God in his hand. This staff had previously served as the instrument of bringing to bear on history the supernatural power of God. In this context, it may be seen as being grasped as a means of drawing down grace and divine strength from God, as a symbol of the prayer of Moses and his connection with the will of God.[13] The efficacy of the prayer prevailed in power and Israel won the victory.

Through this experience the Israelites learned the necessity of maintaining a posture of total dependence upon the absolutely dependable Jehovah, who answered prayer and assured victory in divine power which surpasses the ungodly power of the world.

In Joshua 10:1-23 Yahweh is depicted as the warrior of Israel. This text exhibits how his power worked through his people. It appears that Gibeon was a powerful and royal city (v. 2). The passage states that a peace treaty the Gibeonites had made with Israel alarmed the five Ammonite kings.

---

[10] Hobbs, *2 Kings*, 290.

[11] Hobbs, *2 Kings*, 291.

[12] Robert Jamieson, *Genesis-Deuteronomy* (Grand Rapids, MI: Eerdmans, 1945), 314.

[13] Jamieson, *Genesis-Deuteronomy*, 345.

Due to the perceived threat of alliance, these five kings countered with an alliance of their own: the kings of Jerusalem, Hebron, Jarmuth, Lachish and Eglon joined forces (v. 5). After the Gibeonites heard the news they sent word to Joshua for help. At their request, Joshua immediately acted, assured of God's promised victory: 'The Lord said to Joshua, "Do not be afraid of them; I have given them into your hand. Not one of them will be able to withstand you"' (vv. 8-9). Joshua is quoted as saying, 'Do not be afraid and do not be discouraged. Be strong and courageous. This is what the Lord will do to all the enemies you are going to fight' (v. 25).

An unusual incident occurred when Joshua prayed. He asked the Lord God to extend the daylight and darkness so that Israel could make the most of its victory. In verse 12b, it is noted that Joshua commanded the sun and the moon to 'stand still.' It seems that Joshua spoke in the early morning, because the sun was to the east at Gibeon and the moon to the west over Aijalon (vv. 12-13). The miracle happened as Joshua had prayed. God was in control of all, but yet acted in concert with the voice of his servant.

God was evidently in the midst of the battle. Yahweh was the fighter, the warrior, the victor who crushed the enemy. Verses 9-11 attest that Yahweh caused the enemy to experience panic and confusion. Hailstones killed only Israel's enemies. The victory of the battle did not rest with Joshua but belonged to the One who led the battle. It was obviously a result of the power of God (10:7).

1.3 Punishment

Divine penalty through catastrophe is noted in Exodus 7-11. Moses and Aaron demanded that Pharaoh free the people. Pharaoh rebuffed their appeal because his heart was hardened. Actually, it was God who allowed the hardening so that his astonishing signs and wonders could be displayed against the backdrop of Egypt's ungodly ruler (v. 3).

Exodus 9-11 records the ten diverse plagues brought about by divine power. When Pharaoh discovered his magicians could imitate God's wonders he assumed that Aaron's activity was no more than the magical deception of Egyptian magicians. It is fascinating that the magicians of Egypt performed the same works as Moses and Aaron.

However, God's final plague forced Pharaoh to surrender and obtained the release of the Israelites: 'At midnight the Lord struck down all the firstborn in Egypt, from the first born of Pharaoh who sat on the throne to the firstborn of the prisoner...' (12:29). During the night Pharaoh called on Moses and Aaron and said, 'Up! Leave my people, you and the Israelites! Go, worship the Lord as you have requested' (12:31-32).

In a certain respect, Pharaoh had attempted to determine whether he should observe the source of the power demonstrated by Aaron. So he called his magicians to duplicate the signs.[14]

However, Pharaoh was finally convinced and recognized the power of God, which was unlike the power of the magicians. These awful miracles of judgment proved his solitary, absolute and supreme power over all the gods of Egypt.

In Genesis 12:10-20, when famine occurred in the land where Abram was situated, he did not go back to the place of his birth but rather intended to stay in Egypt. Egypt benefited systematically and extensively applied developments in agriculture.[15] It is a defensible assumption that these amenities attracted Abram and his wife to that prosperous country.

However, Sarai's beauty posed a dilemma. Sarai, coming from a mountainous country, had a fresh and fair complexion compared to Egyptian women who were dark. Thus, Pharaoh was tempted to take her as his wife. This threat rendered Abram helpless to prevent the situation and endangered his own life.[16] Verse 15 says, 'When the officials of Pharaoh saw her, the woman was taken into Pharaoh's house.'

Due to Pharaoh's wrongdoing, God inflicted serious diseases on him and his household. God's divine judgment did not cease in the situation even though Abram had lied, but was demonstrated in his power.

1.4 Other Signs

Exodus 14 tells a tremendous story of God's judgment upon his own people. The Israelites had finally escaped from Egypt and reached the wilderness. Moses was then commanded by the Lord to alter their route slightly. He was told that after staying in Etham north of the sea, the Israelites were to return to the western shore of the sea until they reached their new encampment.[17] The reason for complicating the route seems to have been to decoy Pharaoh, making him think that the Israelites were wandering around the land in confusion and were hemmed-in (v. 3) so that Pharaoh would pursue them (v. 4). God seems to have orchestrated the scene. Yahweh intended to inflict punishment on Pharaoh and his people in the course of their pursuit.

However, upon hearing of the Egyptian's intention to pursue them, the Israelites complained and grumbled against God: 'Was it because there were no graves in Egypt that you brought us to the desert to die?' 'What have you done to us by bringing us out of Egypt?' 'Didn't we say to you in Egypt, Leave us alone; let us serve the Egyptians?' 'It would have

[14] Jamieson, *Genesis-Deuteronomy*, 296.
[15] Jamieson, *Genesis-Deuteronomy*, 132.
[16] Jamieson, *Genesis-Deuteronomy*, 132.
[17] Cassuto, *Book of Exodus*, 159.

been better for us to serve the Egyptians than to die in the desert' (vv. 11-12).

Moses was fully confident in the Lord's deliverance and salvation, even though he did not know in what manner it would come.[18] God's immediate answer to Moses' prayer was the directive to lift up the rod and stretch out his hand over the sea. God caused a strong wind to blow throughout the night and this strong wind divided the sea. Moses' gesture of stretching out his hand demonstrated that this event was an act of God who moves in power to save his people.[19] In general, winds and fire are often used in the Bible to serve as messengers of God of natural phenomena (Ps. 104:4). However, God rescued the Israelites through a magnificent display of his great power.

Exodus 17:1-7 retells the difficult journey of the Israelites in the desert. They suffered due to lack of food. Here they met the problem of the lack of water in the wilderness. In Rephidim, there was little water and they began to grumble. On this occasion, the circumstances were worse than in the two preceding chapters (15 and 16).[20] Because of this critical condition and due to their lack of faith, they rose up against Moses (v. 7). In fact it was an attack on Yahweh.[21]

In response, Moses offered an earnest prayer. God commanded him to strike to rock with the rod that had struck the Nile. The water gushed out of the rock. God replied to Moses majestically. He did not intervene in the relationship between Moses and his people but drew them into the divine focus.[22]

Their thirst caused them to experience continual dependence on a dependable God. The Hebrew word used for 'rock' here is not the same as that used in Numbers 20. The difference between this passage (Ex. 17:1-7) and Exodus 24:11 is that in this instance everyone had enough water, because it gushed out (v. 6); whereas, in Exodus 24:11, the elders alone shared in the divine provision.

The people of God experienced God's power demonstrated in the wilderness. It seemed as if they alone were privileged to encounter this sign.[23] God's mercy and power never ceased, but were continually shown when the Israelites were in need. The extensive power of God was always available to his people.

---

[18] Cassuto, *Book of Exodus*, 159.

[19] Cole, *Exodus*, 121.

[20] Cassuto, *Book of Exodus*, 201.

[21] Durham, *Exodus*, 230.

[22] Cassuto, *Book of Exodus*, 202.

[23] Cole, *Exodus*, 135.

II. Selected Miracle Accounts in the Gospels

2.1 Divine Touch

Luke 17:11-19 recounts the healing of ten lepers. Verse 11 mentions Jesus traveling along the border between Samaria and Galilee. Here the border supplied a fitting location for an event involving both Jews and a Samaritan (v. 16). While Jesus headed into a village, the lepers, standing at a distance, called out for help. Strangely enough, Jesus did not respond to them directly but rather commanded them to go to the priest if they wanted to be healed. He seems to have been testing their faith and obedience. Consequently upon their act of obedient faith, they received their healing.[24]

A conspicuous fact in this case was that one of those healed was a Samaritan. The mercy of the Lord crossed barriers, reached beyond the Jews and touched this Gentile who believed in Jesus' authority. Moreover, this foreigner was the only one who returned to Jesus and expressed his gratitude (v. 15). The Scripture comments that the Samaritan was not only healed but was even saved (v. 19). The word 'made well' may be rendered 'to be saved.'[25] His faith expressed in action led him to receive spiritual salvation.

In John 9:1-7 Jesus healed a blind man who had been sightless his entire life. It raised a question among the disciples, 'Rabbi, who sinned, this man or his parents that he was born blind?' The question about the man's blindness was important in this display of the power and work of God. It was not only a miracle of Jesus but it also signified that Jesus was a light among those living in darkness; it was further proof that Jesus was the long-awaited Messiah (cf. vv. 30-31).[26]

In this instance, Jesus mixed saliva with mud and applied it on the man's eyes, asking him to 'wash in the pool of Siloam' as a way of healing. The method was uncommon.

According to rabbinic tradition, the saliva of the firstborn of a father has healing properties.[27] Having obeyed Jesus, the man opened his eyes and could see (v. 7). The obedience of the blind man, like the faith and obedience of others who were miraculously cured, seems to be regarded by Scripture as a supporting factor of the moving power of Jesus. However, the power itself did not come from obedience nor from the pool but from the One who had authority to heal.

---

[24] Fred B. Craddock, *Luke* (Louisville, KY: Westminster/John Knox, 1990), 203.

[25] Craddock, *Luke*, 203.

[26] D.A. Carson, *The Gospel according to John* (Grand Rapid, MI: Eerdmans, 1991), 363.

[27] Carson, *The Gospel according to John*, 363.

2.2 *Casting out of an Evil Spirit*

Often times Jesus cast out demons from people. The Scriptures declare that only people who have received divine power and Jesus are able to drive out evil spirits. According to Ralph Earle, Luke 4:33-36 specifies two outstanding authorities: authority of teaching and authority over the power of evil.[28] In ancient times, the Jews thought that demons dwelled in deserts, water, air, and subterranean places. When a demon enters a person, according to this belief, the person becomes blind or mute, and various physical and mental disasters plague the person.[29]

A demon-possessed man screamed (Lk. 4:33) while Jesus was teaching in the synagogue. In Greek, 'an unclean spirit' means that he was under its power. This man suddenly acknowledged Jesus, 'the Holy One of God', therefore referring to the Messiah (cf. Jn. 6:69). Then, he pressed further: 'What is there between us?' In other words, 'What is the matter with us?' Earle clearly says that these words denote that the demoniac, or the unclean spirit, was afraid of Jesus. Such spirits were cognizant of the preeminence of divine power. The utterance, 'the Holy One of God', is used in contrast to the demon's own uncleanness.[30]

Jesus looked on the unclean and sullen spirit and rebuked it, 'Be quiet!', which literally means, 'Be muzzled.'[31] The demon with great strength threw the man down before the assemblage and came out without hurting him (Lk. 4:35). This occurrence surprised people and they began to discover the source of this power (v. 37).

Jesus engaged not only in teaching about God but also in demonstrating the power of God. The demon cried out opposing the authority of Jesus. 'The Holy One of God', as uttered by the demon-possessed man, validated the identity of Jesus.

Jesus' exorcism of a demon-possessed boy is shown in Matthew 17:14-18. The boy's life was at stake, for he kept falling into the fire or the water. The father was desperate to rescue his son from demon possession. There was no way to return the boy to normal except through the touch of Jesus Christ. Hence, the father asked Jesus for help. This man addressed Jesus as the Lord, which indicated his recognition of the Messiah (v. 15), and begged for his divine mercy (cf. 8:5; 9:27; 15:22). The father's faith in him seems to be intentionally contrasted in the text with the disciples' little faith (v. 20). The disciples were unable to cast out the demon from the boy due to their lack of faith. The most significant concern of the text seems to be faith.[32] Jesus saw the faith in the father of

---

[28] Ralph Earle, *Mark* (Grand Rapid, MI: Zondervan, 1957), 36.

[29] Craddock, *Luke*, 65.

[30] Earle, *Mark*, 36.

[31] Earle, *Mark*, 37.

[32] D.E. Nineham, *The Gospel of St. Mark* (New York: Seabury, 1968), 242.

the boy and answered his request. He proved himself as a merciful Lord
in this event. The moment 'Jesus rebuked the demon, it came out of the
boy and he was healed' (v. 18). Divine power is displayed in response to
faith.

2.3 Miracles in Nature

Luke 9:10-17 records an extraordinary miracle, the feeding of the five
thousand people. It reminds us that the survival of the Israelites in the
wilderness was dependent upon the awesome provision of God. D. E.
Nineham rightly points out that this was what God performed when he
delivered his people from Egypt. That prominent act of salvation was a
foundational and historical event in Israel.[33]

After hearing the report of the disciples' mission, Jesus took them to a
remote place to avoid the crowd (vv. 1-6). Perhaps Jesus wanted rest from
the crowd to spend time with his disciples in prayer and renewal (Mk.
6:31). But he was not able to evade them. The preaching of the Kingdom
of God was regularly accompanied by healing (Lk. 9:11). Because the
people stayed longer, their stomachs began to grumble. When Jesus heard
about it from the disciples, he ordered the disciples to provide for their
need (Mk. 6:37). He wanted to test their faith (Lk. 8:26). Jesus intended
to show that absolute provision was his responsibility. Finally, Jesus
offered thanksgiving to God and blessed a meager one-person lunch of
bread and fish. Then the miracle occurred as the gathering people
partook of the bread and fish. The food was miraculously multiplied.

Over 5,000 people, including the disciples, had experienced a divine
miracle for the very first time in many of their lives. However, the crowd
may have been expectant since they had heard the accounts of miracles
performed by Jesus. The feeding of the multitude was understood by the
Gospel writers (Mt. 14; Mk. 6; Lk. 9) as one of the essential events of
Jesus' ministry and revelation.

The well known story in Mark 4:35-41 of Jesus calming the sea has
been used in church teaching throughout history. Jesus' power over
nature is vivid and edifying. He proved that he had the ability to control
the sea and subdue storms.[34]

The text says that Jesus and his disciples put out in a boat at night. A
frightening storm arose with strong winds. Jesus lay down and slept in
peace, having faith in God's power to keep him. By contrast, the disciples
were terrified, showing their shallow faith. As the storm threatened, their

---

[33] Nineham, *The Gospel of St. Mark*, 178.
[34] Nineham, *The Gospel of St. Mark*, 146.

terror increased (v. 37). However, their Master illustrated his own trust by sleeping in peace (v. 38). Jesus scolded them for their faltering faith.[35]

Then he was revealed to be sovereign over all nature by rebuking the wind and speaking to the waves, 'Quiet! Be still!' The wind died down and it was completely calm (v. 39). This was awesome to the disciples who had expressed such little faith. Although they had lived and moved with Jesus and had been eyewitnesses of his miracles of healing, and even of raising the dead, they did not fully know how to trust him. Through Christ's demonstration of power the disciples themselves were strengthened in their faith.

2.4 Raising the Dead

Luke 8:49-56 introduces the resurrection of the dead. When Jesus approached the house of Jairus, a synagogue official, a servant met them and said, 'Your daughter is dead. Don't bother the teacher any more' (v. 49). Allan Ironside interprets this as a sorrowful message. Jesus was too late to heal the ailing one. Yet he had been asked by Jairus to do something.[36] Jairus came to Jesus with a passionate heart, believing even that Jesus was able to bring his daughter's life back from death. He believed that the mighty power of Jesus could do anything. Jesus comforted him with the word of hope, 'Fear not: only believe.' The word affirmed to Jairus that the Lord would undertake to resolve this matter.[37] Jesus entered the house and moved with compassion toward the girl. The payroll mourners were ceremonially weeping and wailing to the accompaniment of musicians. Upon looking at her, Jesus said, 'The girl is not dead but asleep.' This did not convince the gathering people. Regardless, Jesus implied that God's power could raise the dead.[38]

To give entire attention to her, Jesus left the crowd outside and was alone with the child. Then he held her hand and spoke, 'My child, get up!' Immediately her spirit came back and at once she stood up. Then Jesus asked the people to give her something to eat (vv. 53-55). The faith of Jairus invited the power of Jesus to grant life back to the girl. The faith of Jarius was essential for Jesus to perform the miracle.

Luke 8:56 (Jn. 11:1-16) recounts the death and resurrection of Lazarus. This took place in Bethany on the east side of the Mount of Olives, less than two miles from Jerusalem, along the road toward Jericho.[39]

---

[35] Richard B. Gardner, *Matthew* (Grand Rapids, MI: Eerdmans, 1991), 151.

[36] Allen H. Ironside, *Gospel of Luke* (Neptune, NJ: Loizeaux Brothers, 1968), 276.

[37] Ironside, *Gospel of Luke*, 277.

[38] Gardner, *Matthew*, 159.

[39] Carson, *The Gospel according to John*, 405.

A sister of Lazarus, Mary, is better introduced to the reader in a later chapter of the book of John when she poured perfume on Jesus' feet and wiped them with her hair (Jn. 12:1-8). Her family was also seen in Luke 10:38 when they lavished hospitality upon Jesus and his disciples and allowed them to rest from their journey. It has been thought that Jesus and Lazarus' family had close fellowship generated by the love of Jesus (v. 3). This love and affection of Jesus is, in fact, one of the key factors motivating Jesus to raise Lazarus. We see his love further displayed when Jesus lingered for a time after the healing.

An important message in this account is that Jesus meant to show God's glory; not only that God would be exalted or praised but also to disclose the glory of God clearly through the Son, Jesus (Jn. 11:40). Through this incident, Jesus accomplished two important things. He demonstrated the power of resurrection and life (v. 25) and he thus generated faith in his disciples (v. 15) to some Jews who were in attendance (v. 45), and to the family of Lazarus itself (v. 22).

III. Selected Miracle Accounts in the Book of Acts

God's powerful miracles are also evident in the book of Acts. The disciples of Jesus, empowered after the infilling of the Holy Spirit, plunged into the world and preached the good news accompanied by divine miracles. Acts 9:36-43 records an account of a resurrection. Peter commanded the dead woman, 'Tabitha, get up' (v. 40). 'She opened her eyes, and seeing Peter she sat up.' This news spread all over Joppa and many people came to believe in Jesus. Acts 19:11-12 notes that God performed extraordinary miracles through his servant Paul. Verse 12 says, 'So that even handkerchiefs and aprons that had touched him were taken to the sick, and their illnesses were cured and evil spirits left them.' When Paul and Silas were thrown into the Philippian prison after being falsely accused of inciting a riot, God's power struck causing an earthquake. The doors were opened and their chains released (16:16-40). Acts 28:3-6 records a snakebite on Paul's hand in Malta. When Paul landed on this island on his way to Rome it was cold and rainy. The islanders built a fire for Paul and the people with him as a gesture of their welcome. Suddenly, a viper came out of the fire and bit Paul's hand. He shook it off and suffered no ill effects. There were many miracles performed during the period of the apostolic mission. Such intense manifestation is continuing as the Holy Spirit works even today.

Some scriptural references in Acts regarding power manifestation are: 4:17-22; 5:17-41; 8:9-24; 9:1-19, 32-35; 13:6-12; 14:1, 3-4, 6, 19; 16:16-23; 19:23-40.

IV. Conclusion

Manifestations of God's power as recorded in the biblical accounts have been discussed in this chapter. I discovered several important purposes of divine manifestation through the study of 'power in mission.' Firstly, they help God's people understand more about God and his greatness. Secondly, the Gentiles in the Old Testament come to know who God is. Finally, unsaved people come to Christ. In the Old Testament God constantly revealed his power, as did Christ in the New Testament as he ministered with power.

Power demonstrations were key in spreading the gospel of the kingdom of God in Bible times as well as essential today among the animists I have been working with. Having been with animistic people who believe in the power of spirits, I have learned that they accept God's power when it is demonstrated on the sick. They have said that God's power is greater than their gods' power, because often the sick one is not healed although a sacrifice has been wholeheartedly offered. Often their hearts are opened during desperate times to hear of a new god. Not only does the sick person turn to Christ through the healing but family, relatives and neighbors come to church. Demonstrations of the healing power of a loving God are instrumental in bringing people to a saving faith and relationship with Jesus. This awareness must extend to the point of experience, beyond head knowledge, as we minister to lost souls.

Miracle Accounts among the Kankana-ey Tribe[1]

The Kankana-eys are a people-group my husband and I have been
working with for fifteen years. Many have come to Christ through
experiences of miraculous healing. Between the years of 1950-70 and at
the present time, the manifestation of the healing gift has been a regular
aspect of worship services. The fact that the Kankana-eys are basically
animists and ancestor worshipers make it easy for them to believe in
God's healing power. They have believed for centuries that the spirits of
the deceased co-habit their houses and communities. Benevolent spirits
are believed to provide healing when a proper ritual is offered. Therefore,
when God's healing power is manifested, especially to those who have
exhausted all means of seeking help from the spirit world, people easily
turn from their religion to Christ. Occasionally whole families and entire
communities have been known to turn to Christ because of divine
healing. This 'people movement'[2] is often a result of God's miraculous
works, especially healing.

Healing of the Spinal Cord

An old man had a severely critical spinal problem so that he could only
crawl on his hands and knees like an animal. His life had been extremely
difficult. He was almost totally abandoned by his friends and relatives;
even his own close family. Long-term sickness or a physical handicap of
a family member often causes those closest to them to fret or be irritated.
Negligence and inattention by the family will frequently hurt the afflicted
one. The Kankana-eys offer numerous sacrifices to the spirits for healing
of physical problems.

---

[1] Julie Ma, 'Manifestation of Supernatural Power in Luke-Acts and the Kankana-ey
Tribe of the Philippines', *Spirit and Church* 4:2 (2002), 109-28.

[2] Alan Tippet, *People Movements in Southern Polynesia* (Chicago, IL: Moody,
1971), 6.

In 1958, Elva Vanderbout conducted a revival meeting[3] in the area where this old man lived. His friends carried him to the neighboring village to attend the revival meeting. The Spirit of God swept among the gathering people so that many were slain in the Holy Spirit. At the end of the meeting, the man was instantly healed: he stood up and began to walk. He immediately surrendered his life to Christ. He walked to the pulpit, showed his upright body to the congregation and told everyone what God had done for him. Such phenomena encouraged many non-believers to come to believe in the Lord.

Healing of a Paralytic

A certain paralyzed woman lived in a mountain village in Benguet Province. She constantly required full attention and care. Literally, she could do nothing for herself, from taking a bath to eating food. Her life was miserable. Family members were busy, working either on farms or in the mines, their primary means of livelihood. They would leave the sick one in a room and go to work.

An opportunity came to attend a revival meeting. While the speaker was praying for her, the Holy Spirit touched her body. She was instantly healed. She rejoiced in the presence of God as she stood and walked through the aisles to the platform and testified to God's healing power. People in the meeting were amazed, and glorified the name of Jesus Christ.[4] Many came to Christ.

Healing of a Deaf-Mute

A girl eighteen years old, who had been a deaf-mute for twelve years, was instantly healed during a night service. She had developed a hearing and speech problem in her early life. Her friends at school in the village teased and ridiculed her. She cried frequently and developed an inferiority complex. As usual, her parents performed rituals with the hope she would be healed, but nothing happened. One day, her mother heard that there was a revival in a village church and people were healed miraculously. When her mother took her to the service, people with various illnesses lined up for prayer.[5] She was in the queue as well. When the worship leaders came to pray for her, she had already felt something unusual. The power of God went through her body and she was healed in

---

[3] She was a single American missionary and was the key person God used to reach the Kankana-ey tribe.

[4] Julie Ma, *When the Spirit Meets the Spirits* (Frankfurt am Main: Peter Lang, 2000), 81.

[5] Ma, *When the Spirit Meets the Spirits*, 80-81.

a flash. Suddenly she was able to hear the noise of the people praying and crying. This miracle brought many pagan neighbors to the Lord.

Healing of a Goiter

One distinguished woman in Baguio City[6] was healed of a huge goiter. She was fairly well-known in the city but had a shame-filled life because of the big mass in her neck. She had tried every possible medicine but all failed. It made her life miserable.[7] Hearing what was happening in the revival meetings held in Baguio City, she made up her mind at once to attend the services. The goiter amazingly shrank when she was prayed for, and by the next service it had totally disappeared. She could not believe what had happened to her. The huge goiter that had hung in her neck for years was gone by the power of God. Since then, she has become a faithful Christian and witness to people at work. This incident also caused many around her to believe in Jesus Christ.

There are other healing accounts. An old man, who had been deaf in both ears since he was a young man, was instantly healed in a revival meeting. At another revival meeting, an old woman who had been blind in both eyes since 1942 was healed and could see in both eyes. A little girl, who was not able to stand on her feet for two years, began to lift up her body and walked by the touch of the Spirit. It was just like the miracles of the early church.

The healing miracles never ceased from the early days of ministry among the Kankana-ey tribe. Christians tend to put strong faith in God once they turn from their traditional religion to Christ. They are also honest in revealing their physical problems although by nature they are introverts. This candid attitude, in fact, encourages the one who prays for them to pray more sincerely. I include some recent miracle accounts below.

Restoration of Eye Sight

In 1975, a woman named Kapeng Andaloy, living in Cabututan Ampusungan, Bakun Benguet, had suffered from physical illnesses for more than ten years. She had lost her eyesight and had hearing problems. Worse, she could not walk. Strangely enough, the physical problems started after her husband's funeral. Then, she developed pain in her knee. Her terrible illness raised the suspicion that her husband's funeral was not properly conducted. However, there was not ample evidence to prove that.

---

[6] Baguio City is located 5,000 feet above sea level and is the only chartered city in the Cordillera. The city has an access to lowland and highland where twelve major tribes live. The city was established in 1905.

[7] Ma, *When the Spirit Meets the Spirits*, 82.

The pastor of a United Church of Christ in the Philippines (UCCP) congregation invited Pastor Tito Inio,[8] a mountain tribal minister in the northern Philippines, and his evangelistic team to conduct a revival meeting. At night, after the service, the pastor requested they visit some houses nearby. In tribal culture, it is common to stop at neighbors' houses and engage in simple conversation. The team sat down in one small house where the woman named Kapeng lived. They began to share the gospel and their testimonies. She paid no attention and was not interested at all. Instead, she kept on saying, 'there is no God, no God.' Later we discovered that two pastors had come to her and prayed for healing, but she had never been healed. Pastor Tito asked a group of people to pray for Kapeng although she was hesitant to be prayed for. However, she joined us in prayer and the intensity of our prayers grew. After quite a while our voices became softer. Then she felt some differences in her body. She was able to hear and see. The pain in her knee had almost disappeared. God instantly healed her. This miracle caused her and her family, in addition to other non-believers in the village, to come to the Lord. Kapeng has been a faithful Christian and attends Bible study.

Healing of a Toxic Goiter

Edna and her family were total pagans. She was born in Malsasin Itogon, Benguet. Since 1997 she had been suffering with a toxic goiter and ulcer and had regular medical check-ups. Although she had been taking medication, she was not getting better but only became worse. Her body became so weak that she could not walk properly. Her family conducted rituals through the help of a village priest. Trying to be cured, Edna found a religion, 'Ama-Ama', which is a combination of spiritism and Catholicism. She was taken to the village of Sayangan for eight months where such religious activity was prevalent. Nothing helped her. The family offered countless sacrifices. The last solution was to put her in a hospital but her doctor declared that he could do nothing for her. At one point, Edna experienced death when she stopped breathing. However, when she was brought to the hospital she was resuscitated.

My ministry team and I visited her home in early spring 1998 but could not minister to her very much, and in the fall we revisited her. Edna was in a critical condition and desperate for any help from anyone. We asked her family and relatives nearby not to offer any sacrifices nor seek any other religions for Edna's healing so that she could be healed by God's power. We told them that if they kept this promise, we would pray for Edna for twenty-one days. However, her mother opposed this

---

[8] He has been in our ministry team for more than ten years.

suggestion. Edna reacted to her mother's resistance by saying, 'We offered so many sacrifices but they never helped me.' After a short argument, they decided to allow us to pray for her. The team members laid their hands upon her sick body and prayed. While we were praying she felt something in her neck and was able to swallow her saliva, which she could not do before. The goiter disappeared in the sight of many witnesses. We returned home and prayed for twenty-one days as promised. When we visited her twenty-one days later, she was able to walk and talk. She attended our first church service. This outstanding incident led many people to the Lord. Edna became a healthy, strong, and faithful Christian.

Healing from a Brain Tumor

There was a child named Gemma living in Benguet Province. She had been sick and bedridden since she was a small child. She often felt dizzy, losing consciousness for several hours. When she regained consciousness, she was extremely exhausted. Gemma was not healthy at birth but now she had been suffering from a brain tumor for nearly two years. On February 14, 2000, the pastor, Tito Inio, met Gemma. He began to pray for her and invited his congregation to join him in prayer for this sick child. The pastor and some of his church members visited her every Monday and prayed for healing. Continual prayer led to her improvement. On June 26, 2000, Gemma started standing and walking slowly. Then, she was able to move her body without help. The next month she could go outside her house alone and talk with her neighbors. Normally she vomited when she ate, but now she could eat without throwing up. While she was struggling with the brain tumor, she lost most of her hair and was almost bald. Miraculously her hair started to grow. Then, the pastor and his church members began to pray for her eyesight to be restored. Constant and intensive prayer created an unusual phenomenon. While she was praying she felt a little light strike her eyes and the light became brighter and brighter.

Gemma's health improved so rapidly that she was even able to assist her mother with cooking. She exercised different parts of her body. With the prayer support of many people, Gemma came to the church's tenth anniversary celebration for Pastor Tito. She testified during the service that she never vomited food nor lost consciousness anymore. Her hair grew fast and was almost as long as many of her friends. Gemma could move her body without hesitation or difficulty. She was very grateful for what God had done for her. Her testimony touched many hearts. Some non-believers, invited particularly for this occasion, heard the wonderful story of God's miracle performed in this child's life. This good news eventually spread to her whole village.

Casting out of Demons

In July 2000, when mountain ministry team members went to Saddle, Itogon, Benguet, they met a man on their way to church. This man freely engaged in conversation with them. As they exchanged more conversation, the team members discovered that his wife, Mylen Codangos, was demon-possessed and had suffered for the past six months. This man, named Codangos, explained that when his church pastor came over and prayed for her, she mocked the pastor and spit on him. He implored the team to pray for his wife. They told him to consult with his own pastor, so that the pastor would not be offended. The leader of the team, Pastor Tito Inio, met with his pastor and they went together to the Codangos' house. It took about fifty minutes to hike there. Finally they arrived and met Mylen, the wife who was tormented by the demon. The team rested a little while then began to pray for her. As they prayed, she screamed at the top of her voice, 'You cannot make us go because she is ours and we continue to control her life.' Then, she started to vomit and shouted for a long time. Finally, she was slain in the Spirit. They continued to pray for complete restoration. While praying, they asked the demons their names. Her voice immediately changed into a man's, saying, 'We are numerous and you cannot defeat us.' Pastor Tito rebuked them by saying, 'You were defeated two thousand years ago by Jesus Christ.' After about an hour of prayer, she became quiet and sat still in a chair. However, they could not cast all the demons out of her and some remained. Several days later, they made a second visit. This time Mylen was completely set free from the bondage of demon possession. She returned to normal and talked to her husband with a smiling face. Since then, both have attended a church in the village. Such power encounters are rather common among people in the villages as they turn to the Lord.

Another Case of Casting out of Demons

A woman named Betty from the mountain village, Labilab, was a domestic helper in Taiwan for two years. During this time, she became demon-possessed and returned to the Philippines. In October 2000, a sectional fellowship was held at Bonifacio Christian Center in Baguio City. The first evening Betty attended the meeting with encouragement from a relative. During the meeting, Pastor Tito Inio was called for. When he entered, Betty, stood by the window and was about to jump out of it. Many became frightened by her radical behavior, and others tried to stop her but to no avail. The meeting paused for a moment due to the commotion. Her relatives and friends could not figure out why she wanted to kill herself. Betty herself probably did not know why she would attempt to jump from twenty feet up. People began to pray and someone slowly pulled her arms back to prevent her from jumping. Prayer continued. Her eyes were sharp and her mouth moved as fast as typing words in a typewriter. After some time of prayer, she began to vomit and bubbles came out of her mouth. Betty's rigid countenance became tender and relaxed. However, Pastor Tito felt the need to pray more. Out of his concern, he asked her relatives to bring her to his church on Sundays. Much prayer was offered for her complete release. Now she attends Bonifacio Assembly of God Church. Betty's total liberation from demon-possession became a living testimony to God and what he has done. It drew many people in her village to Christ.

CHAPTER 5

Mission of Jesus in the Spirit (Luke 4)

The Messiah, after being anointed by the Spirit, ministered primarily among the poor, the blind, and the oppressed (Lk. 4:18-19). Before beginning his actual mission, Jesus the Messiah spent a lengthy time of preparation in the wilderness in prayer and fasting. He returned to Galilee fully empowered, anointed by the Holy Spirit. He was ready to declare the message of the Kingdom of God, demonstrating supernatural power. This chapter will discuss the mission of the Lord in the specific biblical context of Luke 4.

I. The Origin of the 'Year of the Lord's Favor'

Jesus went into the synagogue and opened the Scriptures to Isaiah. Isaiah 61:1-2 declares,

> The Spirit of the Sovereign Lord is on me because the Lord has anointed me to preach good news to the poor. He has sent me to bind up the brokenhearted, to proclaim freedom for the captives and release from darkness for the prisoners, to proclaim the year of the Lord's favor.

Verse 2 mentions the words, 'the year of the Lord's favor.' What is the significance of the year of the Lord ? There is a close connection between the phrases, 'sent me to bind up the brokenhearted' (Is. 61:2) and Leviticus 25:10, 'It shall be a jubilee for you' (in Hebrew *jobel* [jubilee] means a 'blast' of a trumpet, also called the 'year of liberty.' Ezekiel 46:17 translates, 'year of freedom'). Leviticus 25:41 says, 'Then he and his children are to be released.' It is intended to provide a release, 'freedom', or 'liberty', to all Hebrew slaves as well as to the land every fifty years in the year of Jubilee (Lev. 25:10-11).

According to Leviticus 25:39-41, during this year those who were slaves because of their poverty were released. Furthermore, land that was leased due to poverty was to be returned to the original owners (vv. 10-13). Not only that, debts were canceled since it was the year following seven times seven sabbatical years (Deut. 15:1-6). Verse 2 reads, 'because the Lord's time for canceling debts has been proclaimed.' These passages clearly address 'liberty' of the poor during the year of Jubilee.

Isaiah 61 is a prophecy first given to the despondent people of God shortly after the Babylonian exile. While many of the Jews were scattered outside the Promised Land, even the few people who returned from Babylon were continually tormented under 'unrighteous rules.' The righteous continued to wait for the dismissal of the charges.[1]

Encouragement and assurance were proclaimed that God had not forsaken them but rescued them by ushering in 'the year of the Lord's favor.'[2] According to R.J. Dillon, Luke not only quoted from Isaiah 61:1-2 but he quoted a phrase from Isaiah 58:6 between Isaiah 61:1 and 61:2, 'to set the oppressed free', which Luke recorded as, 'to release the oppressed' (Lk. 4:18). I do not find any of the scholarly explanations satisfactory on 'this strange state of affairs.'[3] The underlying assumption is that Luke purposely included this phrase from another chapter of Isaiah to communicate something significant to his readers which was obviously not adequately set out in Isaiah 61.[4] The words 'to set the oppressed free' relate to a uniquely social stance in Isaiah 58. They are spoken in the realm of 'prophetic criticism of social discrepancies in Judah, of the exploitation of the poor by the rich.'[5] Even when fasting the rich never neglected to seek their own pleasure, have their workers labor longer and harder (Is. 58:3), and fight with people who borrowed money from them.[6]

Into this terrible context the prophet Isaiah declared (Is. 58:6-7),

> Is not this the kind of fasting I have chosen:
>   to loose the chains of injustice
>   and untie the cords of the yoke,
>   to set the oppressed free
>   and break every yoke?
> Is it not to share your food with the hungry
>   and to provide the poor wanderer with shelter

---

[1] Donald J. Verseput, 'The Davidic Messiah and Matthew's Jewish Christianity', in Eugene H. Lovering, Jr (ed), *Society of Biblical Literature 1995 Seminar Papers* (Atlanta, GA: Scholars Press), 102-16.

[2] Rainer Albertz, 'Die "Antrittspredigt" Jesu im Lukasevangelium auf ihrem alttestamentlichen Hintergrund', *Zeitschrift für die Neutestamentliche Wissenschaft* 74 (1983), 182-206.

[3] Bosch, *Transforming Mission*, 100.

[4] R.J. Dillon, 'Easter Revelation and Mission Program in Luke 24:46-48', in D. Durken (ed), *Sin, Salvation and the Spirit* (Collegeville, MN: Liturgical Press, 1979), 253-65.

[5] Bosch, *Transforming Mission*, 100.

[6] Albertz, 'Die "Antrittspredigt" Jesu', 193.

> when you see the naked, to clothe him...

The 'oppressed' or 'victims' of this chapter are to be recognized as people who were devastated. Furthermore, those who were bond slaves had no hope of ever escaping from the horrible grip of poverty. Only in a Jubilee, a 'year of the Lord's favor', would they have opportunity to be released from a miserable life.[7] Ethical problems in society were common to the people around Jesus, even if they were not familiar with the 'oppressed' of Isaiah 58:6. Luke 4:18 must, therefore, address the same issue.[8]

A fact to consider is that Jesus' concern for the poor may have been nurtured as he was growing up. Nazareth is a city in Galilee (Lk. 4:14). About ninety percent of the Jews in Galilee may have belonged to the lower class.[9] He may have been referring to his lack of material possessions when he said that he had no dwelling place to lay his head. His disciples and people who followed him were content even in modest living conditions (feeding the 5,000 in Lk. 9:1-17). In fact, Jesus tended to associate with the poor rather than the rich. He demonstrated his tenderness to the poor who were suffering with limited resources and rising debts. The 'year of the Lord's favor' is declared out of his love and compassion for those who endure the bondage of poverty and for people who have been afflicted in the ways described in Isaiah 58.

II. Preparation of the Messianic Mission in the Wilderness

Jesus, led by the Spirit, spent forty days in the desert praying and fasting before beginning his mission. The messianic temptation took place right after the baptism account. In Luke, it played a significant role as the final preparatory event that introduced the ministry of the Messiah to the public.[10] This preparation was very necessary for him to fulfill the work that the Father gave him to do. These passages (Lk. 4:1-14) imply that prayer is an important element in mission preparation. The temptation in this account contrasts with the temptation in Genesis 3. The fall of humanity was through the first Adam who yielded to the temptation of Satan. The last Adam, the Messiah, resisted the temptation of Satan and gave complete obedience to God. After overcoming all the temptations, 'Jesus returned to Galilee in the power of the Spirit' (Lk. 4:14).

---

[7] Bosch, *Transforming Mission*, 101.

[8] Albertz, 'Die "Antrittspredigt" Jesu', 196-97.

[9] John P. Meier, *A Marginal Jew: Rethinking the Historical Jesus* (New York: Doubleday, 1994), I, 148.

[10] Robert H. Stein, *Luke*, New American Commentary: An Exegetical and Theological Exposition of Holy Scripture 24 (Nashville, TN: Broadman, 1992), 144.

Our question regarding the temptation of Jesus is: how was a sinless Messiah tempted? First, we have to understand that as a human being he could be tempted. He was thoroughly human, the Son of man, at the same time he was fully the Son of God. He had human emotion and said, 'I have a baptism to undergo, and how distressed I am until it is completed' (Lk. 12:50). He expressed sympathy: 'O Jerusalem, Jerusalem, you who kill the prophets and stone those sent to you, how often I have longed to gather your children together, as a hen gathers her chicks under her wings, but you were not willing' (Mt. 23:37; Jn. 7:37). He showed his compassion in Matthew 12:32. He was even angry with his disciples when they lacked faith (Mt. 17:17). Jesus expressed gratitude to the Father (Mt. 11:25). He felt tired and thirsty from his journey and sat down by the well (Jn. 4:6, 7; 19:28). Thus, it was only natural for Jesus to be hungry after a forty day fast.

One important lesson is that the Messiah never used the divine power for himself. He was very aware that it was intended for the Kingdom of God and for winning souls. However, when he was tempted, he was tempted as the Son of God. It was affirmed by the voice from heaven and being anointed by the Spirit. Luke 3:22 states, '"You are my Son, whom I love; with you I am well pleased."' The temptations pulled upon the divine affirmation of Jesus' sonship at the baptism. The satanic temptations pointed at this sonship, 'If you are the Son of God...' (Lk. 4:3). On the contrary, he who was directed by the Spirit to fight and defeat the devil took place long before this account (Lk. 1:32, 35; 3:22). Although Luke underscored the physical and spiritual growth of God's Son (Lk. 2:40, 52; cf. Heb. 5:8), Jesus did not gradually grow into his divinity. Rather, it was as God's Son that Jesus received the baptism and temptation.[11]

Robert H. Stein further elaborates:

> The temptations themselves came from external sources, and in all three Jesus was obedient to God's will. The temptations were all messianic in nature and thus should not be seen as a parallel to 1 John 2:16. Jesus was specifically tempted as God's Son. This is most clearly seen in the second and third temptations, but the fact that the temptations were introduced and concluded by 'If you are the Son of God' indicates that all three were messianic in nature.[12]

Why was the Messiah led particularly into the desert and to fast specifically for forty days? The desert is often understood to be a place where one gets in touch with God (Hos. 2:14-15) and it is a dwelling place of demons and wild beasts (cf. Is. 13:21; 34:14; also cf. Mk. 1:13). Forty is a round number (cf. Deut. 8:2, 4; 9:9; Ex. 16:35; 24:18; 34:28; 1

---

[11] Stein, *Luke*, 144.
[12] Stein, *Luke*, 144.

Kgs. 19:8). It brings to mind the forty years the Israelites wandered in the wilderness (Num. 14:34), Moses fasted for forty days (Ex. 34:28; Deut. 9:9) and Elijah traveled forty days and forty nights until he reached Horeb, the mountain of God (1 Kgs. 19:8). The present participle, 'being tempted', denotes the fact that Jesus was tempted throughout the entire forty days and the three particular temptations provided the climax.[13]

The first temptation was to turn stones into bread (Lk. 4:3). The devil attempted to incite Jesus to discontent, impatience and self-centeredness. Why should he have to endure such hunger when he possesses the power to turn the stones into bread? Why should he deprive himself and obey the laws of a common human reality to starve if he can alter it by an authoritative command? This temptation is aimed at the principal requisites for the fulfilment of his profession as Messiah: his awareness of his calling, his faith in God and his self-proclamation.[14]

The Messiah resisted the temptation unreservedly. He knew that he had come to the wilderness by the direction of the Holy Spirit and continued to be led by the Spirit, not by anything else. Jesus rebuked the temptation from the Word of God as written in Deuteronomy 8:3. He clearly proclaimed that he and all human beings are not just dependent on bread but on God, the ultimate source of everything. This particular biblical text declares that God is the ultimate One who can supply human need. He fed the Israelites with manna in the desert and, without his blessing, even bountiful material means will be of no use.

In the second temptation the devil took Jesus to 'a high place and showed him in an instant all the kingdoms of the world.' And he said to him, 'I will give you all their authority and splendor, for it has been given to me, and I can give it to anyone I want to. So if you worship me, it will all be yours' (4:5-7). One can raise the question: is the devil really the possessor and controller of the world? The answer to this question is given in Ephesians 2:2. In this passage Satan is called 'the ruler of the kingdom of the air.' In Ephesians 6:12 it is written, 'For our struggle is not against flesh and blood, but against the rulers, against the authorities, against the powers of this dark world and against the spiritual forces of evil in the heavenly realms.' 1 John 5:19 states, 'The whole world is under the control of the evil one.'

However, God is the ultimate Ruler of all. The devil was aware that Jesus came into the world to build the messianic Kingdom. If Jesus would worship him, Satan suggested that he would give him the kingdoms of the world. Thus, the messianic Kingdom would be established through compromise with the devil. Satan tried to deceive. It was true that because

---

[13] Stein, *Luke*, 146.

[14] Norval Geldenhuys, *The Gospel of Luke*, New International Commentary on the New Testament (Grand Rapids, MI: Eerdmans, 1979), 159.

of Adam's sin of disobedience, the rule of the world was given to Satan by default.[15]

Nevertheless, Satan rules the world under God's sovereignty. God has never abdicated his authority. The truth is that 'the earth is the Lord's, and everything in it' (1 Cor. 10:26). Even the powers of darkness are not able to act without his 'permissive will.'[16] Jesus overcame the second temptation from the Word of God given in Deuteronomy 6:13. Here, in the original Hebrew text 'fear' was used in 'worship.'[17] Jesus resisted by saying, 'Worship the Lord your God and serve him only.'

The third temptation was, 'throw yourself down from here.' Jesus may have been challenged to test his reliance on the Father's protection. The devil even quoted Psalm 91:11-12. However, it was not a complete quotation, the words, 'in all your ways' were excluded.[18] According to rabbinic tradition, 'when the king, Messiah, reveals himself, then he comes and stands on the roof of the holy place.'[19] Based on this tradition, the devil tempted Jesus, telling him that by casting himself down from the top of the temple he would become the Messiah. The implication was that after successfully landing before the crowd, they would recognize his messianic role.[20]

Jesus quoted from Deuteronomy 6:16, which brings to mind the circumstances of the Israelites in Exodus 17:1-7. At Massah and Meribah they tested Yahweh and went against Moses because of a lack of water. They were full of complaints toward Moses. Jesus knew that the devil's offer had nothing whatsoever to do with trusting in the safekeeping and care promised in Psalm 91. He very suitably answered the tempter by quoting Deuteronomy 6:16.

Jesus overcame every temptation with the Word of God and was 'full of the Holy Spirit' (Lk. 4:1). When he resisted with the Word and the power of the Spirit, the devil could not continue. Jesus prepared for his messianic mission not only with prayer and fasting. He also had full knowledge of the Scriptures and spoke the Word of God in the proper context. This complete preparation led him into holistic mission.

III. Source of Mission: The Spirit and the Word

Luke noted the important role of the Spirit in mission. The Spirit descended upon Jesus at his baptism (Lk. 3:21-22) and descended upon

---

[15] Geldenhuys, *The Gospel of Luke*, 160.

[16] Geldenhuys, *The Gospel of Luke*, 161.

[17] Stein, *Luke*, 147.

[18] William Hendriksen, *Exposition of the Gospel according to Luke*, New Testament Commentary (Grand Rapids, MI: Baker, 1978), 238.

[19] Hendriksen, *The Gospel according to Luke*, 239.

[20] Hendriksen, *The Gospel according to Luke*, 239.

the 120 disciples (cf. Acts 1:5). The presence of the Spirit is evident from the beginning of the temptations in the desert continuing throughout Jesus' mission (Lk. 4:1, 14, 18-19, 36). Luke underscored the reference to Jesus' being directed by the Spirit into the desert (cf. Mt. 4:1). In addition, he recorded that Jesus was 'full of the Spirit' (Lk. 4:1). Jesus' victory over the devil was won because he knew the Word and was 'full of the Spirit.' The Spirit's significance in the desert is apparent, and Jesus' experience became a Spirit experience as well. The Spirit enriched Jesus' mission and his entire ministry is to be understood as taking place in the power of the Spirit.

The primary ingredient for the mission paradigm in Luke is the Holy Spirit.[21] Chapter 4 sets this out clearly. Luke also emphasizes that 'the Spirit of mission' is 'the Spirit of power', *dynamis*[22] (4:14, 36). The same Spirit who was with Jesus during the time of the temptation in the wilderness continued in mission in the early church. God called different individuals and empowered them with the Spirit. In Acts 13:9, Paul was filled with the Spirit and followed in his Lord's footsteps. Philip's encounter with the Ethiopian eunuch, for example, is through the agency of the Spirit (Acts 8:29). The conversion of Cornelius, his household, and the gathering Gentiles who were uncircumcised, was established when a second Pentecost took place: the Spirit was poured out even upon the Gentiles (Acts 10:44-48). Peter, who was directed by the Spirit, played a key role in the conversion of Cornelius. The endorsement by the Jerusalem Council of the resolution to baptize Gentiles without prior circumcision is also described as having occurred under the impulse of the Spirit (Acts 15:8, 28).[23] It is the Spirit who charged the worshiping and fasting church of Antioch to set Saul and Barnabas apart for a special commission (Acts 13:2), and it is the Spirit who sent them out (Acts 13:4). The Spirit did not allow Paul to go farther into Asia (Acts 16:6, 9). All these stories highlight the Holy Spirit as the catalyst, leader, and inspirer of mission.

Luke clearly indicates that true mission begins with the Spirit and power (Lk. 4:36). The Spirit is not only the initiator and guiding factor in mission but also the One who releases power (Lk. 4:14). Empowerment leads to boldness to be witnesses. The Spirit who was upon Jesus directed him to be a great witness to God (Lk. 4:18-19) and emboldened his timid disciples. The notion of being directed by the Spirit into mission is applied in a very comprehensive way to the mission of the disciples. They became witnesses of Jesus immediately after being clothed with power

---

[21] L. Schottroff and W. Stegmann, *Jesus and the Hope of the Poor*, trans. Matthew J. O'Connell (Maryknoll, NY: Orbis, 1986), 98.

[22] Bosch, *Transforming Mission*, 114.

[23] Paul Zingg, 'Die Stellung des Lukas zur Heidenmission', *Neue Zeitschrift für Missionswissenschaft* 29 (1973), 200-209.

from on high (Lk. 24:49; Acts 1:8). The same Spirit in whose power
Jesus had gone to Galilee commissioned the disciples into mission.

Roland Allen observes the importance of listening to the Spirit, who is
the source of direction. People who are gospel-bearers pay attention to an
internal Spirit not an external voice. This is beyond human wisdom.
People lead from without whereas Jesus directs from within; people tend
to command but Jesus inspires. Jesus, who received the Spirit, was driven
by the Spirit to work following the nature of the Spirit. This is the central
idea of mission in Luke's teaching on mission.[24]

The Spirit is 'the initiator and the one who empowers to mission.'[25]
Mission is the direct result of the outpouring of the Spirit. Through the
Spirit, God has fulfilled and guided mission.[26] The connection of the
Spirit and mission (Lk. 4:18) is certainly Luke's unique contribution to
the missionary perspective in the early church. Recognition of the work
of the Holy Spirit is acknowledged in different historical periods. David
Bosch elaborates:

> By the second century AD the emphasis had shifted almost exclusively to the Spirit
> as the agent of sanctification or as the guarantor of apostolicity. The Protestant
> Reformation of the sixteenth century tended to put the major emphasis on the work
> of the Spirit as bearing witness to and interpreting the Word of God. Only in the
> twentieth century has there been a gradual rediscovery of the intrinsic missionary
> character of the Holy Spirit. Undoubtedly, Luke did not intend to suggest that the
> initiative, direction, and power of the Spirit in mission applied only to the period
> about which he was writing. It had, in his view, permanent validity.[27]

Therefore, for Luke, the Spirit plays a key role in fulfilling God's will to
save, in the ministry of Jesus, and in the mission of the church to the
world.[28]

Luke 4 denotes the central importance of the Scriptures in the life of
Jesus. His knowledge and understanding of the Scriptures assisted him as
he defeated the devil, as discussed above. In each test, Jesus used the
Scriptures to rebuke the devil. Jesus is the fulfilment of the Scriptures in
the Old Testament. He is not only engaged in mission with the Spirit but
also allied with the Word. Thus he declares the words of God from Isaiah
61:1-2 and 58:6, indicating that his mission in the Spirit will fulfill the

---

[24] Roland Allen, *The Ministry of the Spirit: Selected Writings by Roland Allen*, ed.
David M. Paton (Grand Rapids, MI: Eerdmans, 1962), 5.

[25] Bosch, *Transforming Mission*, 114.

[26] B.R. Gaventa, '"You Will Be My Witness": Aspects of Mission in the Acts of the
Apostles', *Missiology* 10 (1982), 413-25.

[27] Bosch, *Transforming Mission*, 114-15.

[28] Donald Senior, 'The Foundations for Mission in the New Testament', in Donald
Senior and Carroll Stuhlmueller (eds.), *The Biblical Foundations for Mission* (Maryknoll,
NY: Orbis, 1983), 269.

Scriptures. The resources of the messianic mission are the Spirit and the Word.

Jesus manifested the divine power of the Spirit and consistently taught his followers. This implies that knowing the Word is an important aspect of the Christian life. Matthew addresses Jesus' ministry of teaching. Matthew 5-7 display Jesus' deep commitment to the teaching of Kingdom ethics. Jesus is concerned that the lives of Kingdom people be different from non-Kingdom people. Luke 6:20-22,

> Blessed are you who are poor,
>> for yours is the kingdom of God.
> Blessed are you who hunger now,
>> for you will be satisfied.
> Blessed are you who weep now,
>> for you will laugh.
> Blessed are you when men hate you,
>> when they exclude you and insult you
>> and reject your name as evil,
>> because of the Son of Man.

In Acts, Luke emphasizes an important aspect of the ministry of the Word in different regions. The apostles not only demonstrated power through healing and casting out demons but also followed up power ministry by teaching the Word of God. The church in Antioch (Acts 11:19-21) suffered persecution because of Stephen and was scattered as far as Phoenicia, Cyprus and Antioch to preach the Word of God. At the same time believers from Cyprus and Cyrene traveled to Antioch and started to minister to the church the good news of the Lord. Through the proclamation of the Word, great numbers were added to the Kingdom of God. In the church in Berea (Acts 17:11), the attitude of Jesus was formed among the members and they observed the commandments and teachings of the Scripture blamelessly.

Jesus had been raised in this way by his parents (Lk. 2:39, 41). He saw his mission in light of the fulfilment of Scripture (Lk. 4:18, 19) and taught that the way to eternal life lay in obedience to scriptural teaching (Acts 10:25-28; 18:18-22). Obeying Scripture centers around faith in and conformity to the Lord who is the focal point of the Scriptures—Jesus Christ. It would be hard for Luke's readers not to grasp how central and significant the Scriptures are for their Christian life. Jesus, 'full of the Spirit' and full of the Scriptures, is the true model for believers and cross-cultural workers doing mission.

IV. Goal of Mission

The writings of Luke reveal interest in the poor, the neglected, and the marginalized. Throughout the Gospel, the poor caught the attention of Jesus while the rich were left on the outer perimeter. Luke 1:53 reads, 'He has filled the hungry with good things but has sent the rich away empty.' The parable of the rich fool (Lk. 12:16-21), the account of the rich man and Lazarus (Lk. 16:19-31), and the anecdote of Zacchaeus, the chief tax collector of Jericho (Lk. 19:1-10), show the unique focus of Luke. The word *ptochos*, 'poor', appears ten times in Luke, compared to five times in Mark and Matthew. Luke also uses the related terms 'want' and 'need.'[29] Mazamisa notes that,

> [Luke's] concern is with the social issues he writes about: with the demons and evil forces in first century society which deprived women, men and children of dignity and selfhood, of sight and voice and bread, and sought to control their lives for private gain; with the people's own selfishness and servility; and with the promises and possibilities of the poor and the outcasts.[30]

The Old Testament word for the poor refers to both social and religious humility. The poor are, on the one hand, the victims of the unfair structures of society—powerless, unimportant, exploited, economically deprived, and oppressed; but, on the other hand, they are the spiritually devout calmly and entirely trusting in God.[31] The 'poor' hoped for both social and spiritual deliverance. The Law, Prophets, and Psalms declare that 'Yahweh took the side of the poor and oppressed and vindicated their rights against their rich and powerful oppressors.'[32] The Babylonian exile helped to develop the notion of Israel becoming poor. The exoneration of Israel was to be largely eschatological and apocalyptic. The Qumran community considered themselves as the 'poor' waiting for deliverance while collectively storing a communal supply of goods. They regarded the rich and highly educated priestly aristocracy of Jerusalem as their arch-enemies.[33]

This theme is also to be found in Isaiah. The word *anawim* of Isaiah 61:1 is quoted and translated in Jesus' proclamation as the *ptochoi* (poor) in Luke 4:18. Luke employs this term for the poor in the identical and larger respect of *anawim* referring to both the socially and spiritually poor. The social aspects of the term 'poor' are emphasized in Luke's

---

[29] James A. Bergquist, '"Good News to the Poor"—Why Does This Lucan Motif Appear to Run Dry in the Book of Acts?', *Bangalore Theological Forum* 28 (1986), 1-16.

[30] L.W. Mazamisa, *Beatific Comradeship: An Exegetical-Hermeneutical Study on Luke 10:25-37* (Kampen: Kok, 1987), 37.

[31] Meier, *A Marginal Jew*, I, 384-85.

[32] Meier, *A Marginal Jew*, I, 385.

[33] Meier, *A Marginal Jew*, I, 385.

writing, obviously in the Beatitudes where the poor are compared with the rich. The reasons to stress the discrepancies between the rich and the poor are that they generally correspond to the socio-economic actualities in the church. Thus, in general, the poor tended to accept the message of the Kingdom while the rich rejected it.[34]

Jesus came 'to preach good news to the poor' but also 'to proclaim freedom for the prisoners and recovery of sight for the blind, to release the oppressed.' The Messiah was portrayed as mankind's hope in the earliest Christian church and today. People who are in darkness will be set free, they will see the light of day, and their eyes will be opened.[35] One reason that the Messiah was sent into the world is to open people's eyes (Jn. 9:39a).

John's writings provide spiritual dynamism for the above subject. One primary example is associated with the account of the Samaritan woman at the well (4:7-42). In this actual setting he crossed racial boundaries and religious issues that kept the Jews and Samaritans apart. Jesus' purpose was to accept her. He raised her interest and created a hunger for his answers to her social and spiritual needs. He used water to illustrate 'living water' then highlighted a 'gift of God' from the 'living water.' This conversation opened her eyes to a need she had been unaware of in the past.[36] This was a moment of truth for her. She would find the solution to problems she had struggled with her entire life.

Jesus portrayed himself as the 'indispensable solution, the true Savior, the all-sufficient God.'[37] He is the only one who can liberate and rescue those who are under dark powers and spiritual oppression. Jesus claims divine power through which one can overcome temptation (Jn. 8:34-36). Jesus is a Giver of peace to the troubled heart (14:27), is an Encourager to the lonely (14:18; 16:7), and is a true Light to those in darkness (8:12). Above all, he is the eternal life to those in fear, sickness and trembling in death (11:25-26).

Jesus' true love, power and forgiveness release those who are under the bondage of darkness, imprisoned in social injustice and unfairness. He wrought a great freedom to bring deliverance socially and spiritually. The messianic mission is so broad that everyone, no matter what condition they are in or who they are, can come to the Lord and gain true liberation and fulfilment.

---

[34] Robert Guelich, *The Sermon on the Mount* (Waco, TX: Word, 1982), 70.

[35] Hendriksen, *Exposition of the Gospel according to Luke*, 253.

[36] Glasser, *Kingdon and Mission*, 188.

[37] Glasser, *Kingdon and Mission*, 188.

V. Who are Target People?

Luke obviously had a complete theological understanding of God's mission to the Jews and Gentiles.[38] Luke 4:16-30, including the Nazareth episode, records indications of Jesus' ministry to the Gentiles in the future. Jesus grew up in Nazareth, which was situated in a fertile farming region of Galilee[39] where diverse ethnic groups of people lived. Donald Kraybill writes regarding Galilee:

> Galilee, sixty miles to the north of Jerusalem, was the center for the common folk. Rich in resources, Galilee was the most densely populated place of Palestine. Before the reign of Herod the Great, many Gentiles bought land there. But in the years before Jesus' birth, Jewish immigrants resettled in it. By the time of Jesus' birth, Galilee was predominantly Jewish. Herod Antipas, the ruler of the area, built the capital city of Tiberias along the Sea of Galilee. The region, however, still carried its former stigma: 'Galilee of the Gentiles.'[40]

This environment motivated Jesus to include the Gentiles as a people group to reach. The ministry of Jesus expanded into three areas: Galilee (Lk. 4:14–9:50), from Galilee to Jerusalem (Lk. 9:51–19:40), and lastly in Jerusalem. 'Luke does not mention any appearances of the risen Christ in Galilee—everything is concentrated in Jerusalem.'[41]

In the Old Testament, God appears not only as the God of Israel but also as the God of the Gentiles. The fact is that the prophet Elijah had bestowed God's favor upon a Gentile woman in Sidon, and Elisha cured a leper, Naaman, a Syrian. God is not irrevocably bound to Israel. God reveals himself as the universal God and Luke considers Jesus' mission as universal in intention. In fact, the gospel of Jesus was first given to the Jews but they refused, then the good news was brought to the Gentiles.[42] The Nazareth account has a clear Gentile mission orientation and serves to emphasize the basic thrust of Jesus' overall mission at the time of his initial appearance in public.[43]

When dining in the house of a Pharisee, Jesus advised the host to invite to a banquet those who were not able to repay his hospitality, particularly 'the poor, the crippled, the lame, and the blind' (Lk 14:1-14). Jesus attempted to challenge the exclusivist group who never included

---

[38] Stephen G. Wilson, *The Gentiles and the Gentile Mission in Luke-Acts* (Cambridge: Cambridge University Press, 1973), 239.

[39] Donald B. Kraybill, *The Upside Down Kingdom* (Waterloo, ON: Herald, 1990), 79.

[40] Kraybill, *The Upside Down Kingdom*, 78.

[41] Bosch, *Transforming Mission*, 88.

[42] Jacques Dupont, *The Salvation of the Gentiles: Essays on the Acts of the Apostles* (New York: Paulist, 1979), 21.

[43] Eugene A. LaVerdiere and William G. Thompson, 'New Testament Communities in Transition', *Theological Studies* 37 (1976), 589, 593.

unfortunate people. Jesus also urged them to participate in a future reward through inviting those who are ordinarily excluded. Then Jesus presented a parable of a wonderful feast to which those who received an invitation made excuses not to attend. In the parable, the one who extended the invitation was angry and commanded his servant to immediately go into the streets and bring in the poor, the blind, the crippled and the lame (Lk. 14:21). The house owner sent his servant out again to bring additional people to fill the house (Lk. 14:23). The parable concluded with the proclamation that not one of those who were invited will be allowed to join the banquet (Lk. 14:24).

Besides indications of 'an eschatological reversal between those who exclude and those who are excluded', the inclusive idea of the banquet in which people come from afar notes the incorporation of Gentiles into God's mission. This parable also implies that jubilee mission is already and not yet, both present and future. The coming Kingdom of God has begun in the present and created the eschatological jubilee, a serious challenge to the 'status quo' and an order in the continuing practice of Jesus' mission.[44]

Zechariah's hymn (Lk. 1:68-69) implied that Jesus' mission would focus on the Jews: 'Praise be to the Lord, the God of Israel, because he has come and has redeemed his people. He has raised up a horn of salvation for us in the house of his servant David.' Simeon, a righteous man, 'was waiting for the consolation of Israel' (Lk. 2:25). He praised God for 'salvation' and for 'a light for revelation to the Gentiles and for glory to your people Israel' (Lk. 2:30-32). The prophetess Anna, who stayed in the temple and worshiped all day long 'fasting and praying', gave 'thanks to God and spoke about the child to all who were looking forward to the redemption of Jerusalem' (Lk. 2:38). The two travelers to Emmaus, who were engaged in a conversation on the death of Jesus, make an important theological statement: 'but we had hoped that he was the one who was going to redeem Israel' (Lk. 24:21). The disciples shared the same hope as the two men traveling to Emmaus. In Acts 3:19, Peter addressed a Jewish crowd, 'Repent, then turn to God, so that your sins may be wiped out, that times of refreshing may come from the Lord, and that he may send the Christ, who has been appointed for you—even Jesus.' In the first chapter of Acts (1:6) the disciples inquire of the risen Jesus, 'Lord, are you at this time going to restore the kingdom to Israel?' Ample Scripture references provide an indication of Jesus' redemptive work with the Jews.

The emphasis on salvation for the Jews and their theological preference is never separated from the Gentiles and God's mission to them. The

---

[44] Paul Hertig, 'The Jubilee Mission of Jesus in the Gospel of Luke' (unpublished paper, 1997), 11.

Gentile mission is not second to the Jewish mission. Neither is the one simply a result of the other. Rather, the Gentile mission is connected to the Jewish mission. It is not appropriate to say that the Gentile mission only became conceivable after the Jews had deserted the gospel.[45]

VI. Conclusion

The mission of the Messiah teaches the importance of preparation for mission. Preparedness consists of two components: intensive prayer and fasting. Anointing comes and the 'fullness of the Spirit.' Thus, mission is not fulfilled through human agency but through the Spirit. Jesus declared the purpose of his mission to the blind, the poor, the prisoners, and the oppressed, both Jews and Gentiles and that includes both the spiritual and physical dimensions. His holistic mission developed in three different stages: the Gentiles in Galilee, then into Jerusalem and continuing works in Jerusalem. Jesus spent most of his time in Jerusalem. Dillon notes that Christian mission had its 'beginning from Jerusalem', an essential place. Thus, 'beginning' was not just a geographical issue.[46]

Jesus regarded the Word and the Spirit as significant sources for his mission. He vividly demonstrated his unlimited biblical knowledge of the Old Testament and used the Scriptures in his time of temptation. The Word of God was, indeed, a great weapon to overcome Satan's attack. Spiritual warfare in mission, and the empowerment of the Spirit, gave strength and power. Undoubtedly these sources are the core factors in mission. Messianic universal mission encompasses a wide range and different groups of people. His openness to all levels of society is a prime example to us. His inclusive mission goes beyond human interpretation of the *Missio Dei*.

---

[45] Ferdinand Hahn, *Mission in the New Testament*, trans. Frank Clarke (London: SCM, 1965), 134. Jack T. Sanders, 'The Parable of the Pounds and Lucan Anti-Semitism', *Theological Studies* 42 (1991), 667.

[46] Dillon, 'Easter Revelation and Mission Program in Luke 24:46-48', 253-65.

CHAPTER 6

The Great Commission: Church Mandate

The death of Jesus Christ did not totally fulfill the mission of God (*Missio Dei*). The mission was entrusted to the disciples. After his resurrection, Jesus appeared among the gathering disciples who were terrified and had lost hope since their Master's death. However, the hope of salvation for all humanity began to blossom through his disciples as they implemented the Great Commission. The mission of God continues through the church until Christ returns.

I. Jesus' Mission in Matthew: Holistic Approach to Mission

Matthew underscores the mission of Jesus among the Gentiles as well as the Jews. He recorded specific accounts of Jesus' mission (e.g., 8:10; 15:28). Jesus' Gentile mission is also foreshadowed in John 2:13-17; the cleansing of the forecourt of the temple, which was known as the forecourt of the Gentiles, shows that God's salvation was ready for Gentiles. John 2:13-17 implies 'Jesus' spontaneous willingness to enter Gentile homes.'[1] Jesus fulfilled the prophecy of Isaiah that is recorded again in Matthew 4:15-16. Describing the geographical location, it is written, '...Galilee of the Gentiles, the people living in darkness have seen a great light; on those living in the land of the shadow of death a light has dawned.' After the resurrection, Jesus met his disciples in Galilee to commission them to go to the nations (Mt. 28:16-20). David Bosch outlines Jesus' Gentile mission:

> the identification of Galilee as 'Galilee of the Gentiles' (4:15; at the end of the gospel it is again in Galilee, semi-Gentile territory to Matthew, that the disciples are commissioned); the summary of Jesus' activities in 4:23-25, which adds that news about him 'spread throughout all Syria' (in 9:35-38 Matthew has an almost identical summary, where he adds Jesus' word about a plentiful harvest, an obvious allusion to a wider mission; again, Matthew's readers [in Syria] could not have overheard the assertion that the earthly Jesus had been known in Syria); the

---

[1] Bosch, *Transforming Mission*, 61.

reference to the disciples as the salt of the earth and the light of the world (5:13-14f.).[2]

From the beginning of Jesus' earthly ministry, the Gentiles were in his plans and on his mind.

Jesus demonstrated his concern for his own people in Matthew 10. He expressed a restriction in his mission when he said, 'Do not go among the Gentiles or enter any town of the Samaritans. Go rather to the lost sheep of Israel' (vv. 5-6). This statement certainly implied that Jesus focused his mission predominantly on his own and, thus, wanted his disciples to turn their attention to 'the lost sheep of Israel' in the same way.

In Matthew 15:24 Jesus said to the Canaanite woman, 'I was sent only to the lost sheep of Israel.' It expressed the mind of Jesus toward the Gentile mission. However, when she finished pleading Jesus granted her desire. This indicated the unlimited scope of Jesus' mission. The Messiah's mission to Israel and to the Gentiles was not to exclude but rather that they embrace one another.[3] According to Hahn, 'the metaphor of two concentric circles (the larger one signifying the Gentile mission, the other the mission to Israel) which necessarily belong together but, of course, in such a way that the Gentile mission became the all-embracing and over-arching one.'[4]

II. The Women's Task (Matthew 28)

Mary Magdalene and the other Mary came to the tomb at dawn (Mt. 28:1) to care for the body of Jesus. While they were still at the tomb a strong earthquake occurred and the Lord's angel appeared before them. The angel's role was threefold: 1) he rolled away the stone so that the emptiness of the tomb could be seen; 2) he appeared to the guards and let them see that the body was no longer there; and 3) he commissioned the women to go to the disciples and tell them of the resurrection of Jesus Christ (v. 7).

The angel's ultimate purpose was to direct the women to become messengers to the disciples. Jesus could have directly shown himself to the disciples without using the women but he chose this unique way to inform the disciples of his resurrection. Of course, it was quite unusual to employ women during this period. They were not highly viewed or esteemed. These two were told to tell the disciples two things: first, Jesus 'has risen from the dead', and, second, he 'is going ahead of you into Galilee' (v. 7). The meeting place was foretold before his death (26:32). The angel told them to affirm to the disciples that 'he is going ahead of'

---

[2] Bosch, *Transforming Mission*, 61.
[3] Bosch, *Transforming Mission*, 60.
[4] Hahn, *Mission in the New Testament*, 127.

them "into Galilee."' 'The use of the present tense for a future event makes it more vivid and certain.'[5]

The women hastily went from the tomb to the designated place. Sorrow caused by Jesus' death turned to great joy because he was risen. The incredible news of the Master's victory over death was on its way to the disciples. Then, why did Christ expect to meet his disciples in Galilee? The second message, that he was 'going ahead of' them 'into Galilee' and that he would see them there implied a certain reason and purpose. In Matthew 4:20 the words 'Galilee of the Gentiles' underscores the fact that God's mission to the Gentiles intensified from the time of the resurrection.[6]

Obviously for the women, encountering Jesus was a great blessing. They were the last at the cross and the first at the tomb and now they were the first to experience the joy of seeing their Lord. When they saw him, they rushed to their Master and 'clasped his feet and worshiped him' (v. 9). Taking hold of his feet symbolically acknowledged Christ's kingship and was an act of homage.[7] Eventually, the faithful women were the first messengers to proclaim the good news of the resurrection of Jesus.

III. 'Galilee' (Matthew 28:16)

There were eleven disciples of Jesus and two women. They, who were given the Commission on the Mount, became the prime instruments of church expansion in the book of Acts.

By gathering in 'Galilee' the disciples would remember Jesus' earthly ministry and their involvement with him as well. At this meeting in Galilee, the disciples returned to their starting point (4:15-16) while, at the same time, it was the identical place where their lives were thrust onto a worldwide stage. Thus, reuniting at the mountain in Galilee was very significant. Their commissioning recalled many scenes on the mountains: the temptation in 4:8; the Sermon on the Mount in 5:1; the Gentile supper in 15:29; the Transfiguration in 17:1; and the revelation about the end of the world in 24:3.[8]

Jesus spoke about the final revelations of the gospel. 'As it were, the same divine law swings itself like a bow from the mount of the first revelation in Sinai to this mount of the last revelation in Galilee.'[9] Bruner further comments that 'Matthew's Jesus, the New and Better Moses, the

---

[5] Leon Morris, *The Gospel according to Matthew* (Grand Rapids, MI: Eerdmans, 1992), 738.

[6] Morris, *The Gospel according to Matthew*, 738.

[7] Morris, *The Gospel according to Matthew*, 739.

[8] Craig L. Blomberg, *Matthew*, New American Commentary: An Exegetical and Theological Exposition of Holy Scripture (Nashville, TN: Broadman, 1992), 430.

[9] F.D. Bruner, 'Matthew', *Dialogue* 34 (1995), 312-20.

Messiah-Interpreter of God's Law, will give his church her final orders from the Mount of the Great Commission.'[10] Galilee was not only a geographical place but also a theological mark and missiological location; the very founding point of mission. The Great Commission is the key to Matthew's understanding of the mission of Jesus.[11]

IV. 'All Authority' (Matthew 28:17)

Authority seems to be a favorite word in Matthew's description of Jesus (cf. 7:29; 8:9; 9:6; 10:1; 21:23, 24, 27). It conveys the weight of 'deity' and implies ruling power. The authority used by Matthew referring to Christ was translated from the Greek word *exousia,* meaning 'right or power.' By declaring himself as the highest and only authority, Jesus alone stood behind the command of Matthew 28:19.[12] In fact, Jesus gave authority to his twelve disciples 'to drive out evil spirits and heal every disease and sickness' (Mt. 10:1). His disciples had already experienced a foretaste of the divine authority of their Master.

When Jesus declared his absolute ruling power, not only in heaven with God but on earth with men, it meant that he was the central ruling officer of the cosmos, in perfect leadership of the world.[13] Here, 'in heaven' meant that the possibility of salvation (19:26), demanding obedient faith, could be supplied from on high by the One who had authority and who gave the power of 'access.' 'On earth' meant that Christians should fear no human power because of their alliance with the King. 'There was nothing which had power that was not granted by him.'[14]

All authority referred to all the spiritual, religious, social, political and economic power in his hands. 'The kingdoms of this world have become the kingdom of our God and of Christ.'[15] The whole world was in his hands and at his feet because he was and is the Lord of lords and King of kings who shall reign forever and ever. Ephesians 1:19-23 notes,

> his incomparably great power for us who believe. That power is like the working of his mighty strength, which he exerted in Christ when he raised him from the dead and seated him at his right hand in the heavenly realms, far above all rule and authority, power and dominion, and every title that can be given, not only in the present age but also in the one to come. And God placed all things under his feet and

---

[10] Bruner, *Matthew,* II, 1091.

[11] Benjamin Jerome Hubbard, *The Matthean Redaction of a Primitive Apostolic Commissioning* (Missoula, MO: Scholar's Press, 1974), 98.

[12] Peter F. Ellis, *Matthew: His Mind and His Message* (Collegeville, MN: Liturgical Press), 23-24.

[13] Bruner, *Matthew,* II, 1094.

[14] Bruner, *Matthew,* II, 1095.

[15] Bruner, *Matthew,* II, 1095.

appointed him to be head over everything for the church, which is his body, the fullness of him who fills everything in every way.

Christ's exaltation, through his resurrection, implies that one day 'every knee' will bow and 'every tongue confess that Jesus Christ is Lord' (Phil. 2:9-11). Due to this authority, Jesus held the right to send his disciples into the world and he enabled them to carry out his commands. Apparently, this authority has also been given to all believers who obey the Great Commission in the earth.

V. 'Go and Make Disciples' (Matthew 28:19)

The primary instruction in the commission of Jesus is to 'make disciples' (*matheteusate*). Without going it is impossible to make disciples. Karl Barth stated that disciple-making is the way others become as the disciples. Therefore, the communities of believers were continually being refreshed, as the converts themselves became new disciples, and declared the good news of Jesus. Barth emphasized that the Great Commission was not only the proclamation of the gospel but also the making of disciples.[16]

Matthew used the imperative of the verb 'go' three other times in this Gospel as a mandate for people to literally 'go' somewhere (2:8; 11:4; 28:7).[17] Barth interprets 'go' in an interesting way. 'Going points to Christ's kingly rule over the nations.'[18] This indicates that going to different places to proclaim the good news is a job of the representatives of the King and only through the fulfilment of this work will the Kingdom of God and rule of the King be spread.

Discipleship is a main theme in Matthew. The word 'disciples' indicates Matthew's particular ecclesiological emphasis. 'Disciples' appears seventy-three times in Matthew, forty-six times in Mark, and thirty-seven times in Luke. The similar verb of the noun 'disciples', *matheteuein* 'to make disciples', is only seen four times in the New Testament, three of these in the Gospel of Matthew.[19] The resurrection of Jesus pointed to the last mandate of his mission. It includes more than proclamation, requiring submission to the Lordship of Jesus through the making of disciples.[20]

The word 'disciple' identifies believers with Jesus. The disciples of Jesus share his hardships and missionary authority. However, Jesus

---

[16] Waldron Scott, *Karl Barth's Theology of Mission* (Downers Grove, IL: InterVarsity, 1978), 17.

[17] Blomberg, *Matthew*, 431.

[18] Scott, *Karl Barth's Theology of Mission*, 17.

[19] Bosch, *Transforming Mission*, 73.

[20] Bosch, *Transforming Mission*, 232.

himself is Lord, the Son of God, worthy to be praised, and the One to be exalted. Mission, therefore, is not just triumphalist conquest of enemy territories, but is established in humility and servanthood as exemplified in the suffering Servant (Is. 53). The disciples were rather puzzled on the mountain in Galilee and Matthew wanted his readers to be aware that mission never occurs in 'self-confidence' but frailty. Mission happens in a moment of crisis when peril and chance come together.[21]

This was evident to the gospel bearers in the term 'go.' One little word cast out churchly segregation and helped remind its hearers that 'in its mission the church constituted a resistance movement against every manifestation of fatalism and quietism.'[22] Those who would obey God must actively pass his word to other peoples and societies in order to change the world.

Making disciples does not mean simply bringing new church members into a congregation, nor does it mean increasing the church numerically. The discipleship that Matthew writes of is costly. Disciples are encouraged both to understand Jesus' teachings and to fulfill them without compromise (Mt. 7:24-27). Jesus' mission command is more than preaching. Disciple-making is about one's character and life change. It could only refer to the course of transformation into Christ-likeness, as revealed by Jesus' own model of making disciples. Disciple-making is not an accomplishment; it is complete surrender to God's reign.[23]

VI. 'All Nations' (Matthew 28:19)

'All nations' is the translation of *panta ta ethne*. The two primary options for translating *ethne* are as Gentiles (non-Jews) and as peoples (somewhat comparable to ethnic groups). The former interpretation was commonly accepted among those who felt that either Jesus or Matthew understood the fact that God had 'once-for-all' rejected the Jews.[24]

Bosch points out that the 'all nations' of Matthew is used four times, and all of these are in the last portion of his Gospel (24:9, 14; 25:32; 28:19). This is where the Gentile mission comes more clearly into focus. 'The various parallels to Matthew's fourfold use of *panta ta ethne* also evoked universalist imagery: *hole he oikoumene* (the whole inhabited world), *holos (hapas) ho kosmos* (the whole [human] world) and *pasa he ktisis* (the entire [human] creation).'[25] It is apparent that Matthew was

---

[21] Bosch, *Transforming Mission*, 346.

[22] Bosch, *Transforming Mission*, 400.

[23] Paul Hertig, 'The Great Commission Revisited: The Role of God's Reign in Disciple Making', *Missiology* 29:3 (July 2001), 347.

[24] D.R.A. Hare and D.J. Harrington, '"Make Disciples of All the Gentiles" (Mt. 28:19)', *Catholic Biblical Quarterly* 37 (1975), 359-69.

[25] Bosch, *Transforming Mission*, 64.

attempting to say that Jesus was no longer sent only to the chosen but also had become the Savior of all humanity. If Matthew had intended that his audience ('many of whom were Jews, still part of the wider Jewish community') understand that the Jews could no longer be recipients of the gospel, he would have had to state it much more unambiguously. 'An unbiased reader of chapters 24 to 28 of his Gospel can only understand them to suggest that Matthew's concern was with all of humankind, including the Jews.'[26]

Although Matthew observed the cold-heartedness of the Jews, he did not doubt the ongoing efficacy of a mission to his own people. This leaves the 'inalienable task of himself and his community; they continue to regard themselves as inwardly and outwardly tied to Israel. Yet at the same time Jesus is committed to the Gentile mission.'[27]

The phrase 'all nations' refers to all the nations of mission. This phrase is ground into the heart of Old Testament revelation and recalls the promise to Abraham that all the families of the earth shall be blessed through him (Gen. 12:1-3). This blessing which gives 'all the families the ground' is one wherein the blessing of Abraham will 'unite the divided families, and change the curse, pronounced upon the ground on account of sin into a blessing for the whole human race.'[28] This blessing came through Jesus Christ. Galatians 3:16-18 affirms

> The promises were spoken to Abraham and to his seed. The Scripture does not say 'and to seeds', meaning many people, but 'and to your seed', meaning one person who is Christ. What I mean is this: The law, introduced 430 years later, does not set aside the covenant previously established by God and thus do away with the promise. For if the inheritance depends on the law, then it no longer depends on a promise; but God in his grace gave it to Abraham through a promise.

Jesus' 'all nations' greatly inspired the disciples; it meant the worldwide spread of mission and the conversion of peoples from different nations. The mission of discipling all nations to follow Jesus will never cease to be the 'life-program of all those for whom Jesus is Lord.'[29] The resurrected Jesus courageously sent his disciples to 'all nations.' 'The reign of God has been entrusted to God's new people' (cf. 21:43).[30]

---

[26] Bosch, *Transforming Mission*, 64.

[27] Bosch, *Transforming Mission*, 64.

[28] C.F. Keil and F. Delitzsch, *The Pentateuch*, Commentary on the Old Testament 1, trans. James Martin (Grand Rapids, MI: Eerdmans, 1978), 193.

[29] Bruner, *Matthew*, II, 1098.

[30] Bosch, *Transforming Mission*, 65.

VII. 'Baptizing' (Matthew 28:19)

When people became disciples they were to be established in a community; they were to be 'baptized.' This word in the New Testament and in this passage describes being located in the 'triune name.' It means 'identification with.' The phrase 'into the name of' was used to mean 'to the account of.'[31]

Through baptism, people join 'into the account' and 'into the possession of the great God'; baptized Christians come under new guidance. They are moved to a new 'company', into the association of those who honor and worship God the Father, Jesus Christ and the Holy Spirit.[32]

'Baptism' in the Great Commission was to be more than an 'initiating ceremonial, it was sacramental and effectual. And it was empowering and connecting.' It would be appropriate to rephrase 'baptizing them' into 'empowering them into the possession of the loving Father, the life-giving of the Son, and the power of the Holy Spirit.'[33]

Barth interpreted this to mean that 'baptizing reflected the priestly function of objectively introducing others into the realm of God's reign.'[34] The ceremony of 'baptism' seemed to be an important bridge into the 'realm of God's reign.' Baptism was an important way in which the disciple declared to the world that he or she had been drawn into the 'realm of God's reign' or the 'possession of God.'[35] Baptism, therefore, is a moment of change into a realm of belonging.

VIII. 'Teaching' (Matthew 28:19)

The last element of the 'Great Commission' is teaching. Essentially, 'teaching them', and 'baptizing them', is 'disciple-making.'[36]

Three phrases in the 'Great Commission' epitomize the core of mission in Matthew: make disciples, baptize, and teach. Mark employs 'proclaim' (kerysso) and 'teach' (didasko) as synonyms, whereas Matthew constantly separates the two activities.[37] In Matthew, 'preach' or 'proclaim' invariably point to non-believers; they are often used with the phrase 'the gospel of the kingdom.' The injunction to 'proclaim the gospel' (of the kingdom) is also used with distinct 'reference to a future

---

[31] Gerhard Kittel and Gerhard Friedrich, *Dictionary of the New Testament*, Abridged in one volume by Geoffrey W. Bromiley (Grand Rapids, MI: Eerdmans, 1985), 92.

[32] Bruner, *Matthew*, II, 1100.

[33] Bruner, *Matthew*, II, 1100.

[34] Scott, *Karl Barth's Theology of Mission*, 17.

[35] Bruner, *Matthew*, II, 1102.

[36] Bosch, *Transforming Mission*, 65.

[37] Wolfgang Trilling, *Das wahre Israel: Studien zur Theologie des Matthaus-Evangeliums*, 3rd ed. (Munich: Kosel-Verlag, 1964), 150.

(Gentile) mission' (Mt. 24:14; 26:13; cf. 10:7). Jesus did not 'preach' to his disciples and his followers. In the synagogues, Jesus never 'preaches' but always 'teaches.' However, Matthew used 'preach' nine times, 'proclaim the gospel' four times, and 'evangelize' once. Why did he not use the term 'preach' in a 'universal outreach'?[38] Bosch states clearly,

> Behind his choice of terms there are important theological [read: missiological] considerations. To appreciate these, it is important to recognize that, for Matthew, teaching is by no means a merely intellectual enterprise (as it often is for us and was for the ancient Greeks). Jesus' teaching is an appeal to his listeners' will, not primarily to their intellect; it is a call for a concrete decision to follow him and to submit to God's will.... What the apostles should 'teach' the new disciples according to Matthew 28:20, is to submit to the will of God as revealed in Jesus' ministry and teaching.[39]

Although the Great Commission does not specify teaching, based on the great commandment of Jesus, 'love your neighbor as yourself' (Mt. 19:19; 22:39), teaching should be associated with love. Here, neighbor in a broad respect refers to different ethnic groups and an entire world. From the very beginning of human creation, God demonstrated his love through his forgiveness of Adam and Eve. He has constantly revealed his universal love through the history of Israel.

If we declare that we love our neighbors, we cannot help but share the good news of salvation with them. Stott says that within the holistic perspective of mission our neighbor is 'neither a bodyless soul' that we need care for only the soul, 'nor a soulless body' that we need be concerned for its comfortable life alone, but both soul and body are to be attended.[40] We go as Jesus did, into the world in love and offer our own lives. An act of loving people who 'go' draws others to follow Jesus and obey his will, which is required for Kingdom people.

'Teaching them to obey everything' was a 'safeguard built into the commission which protected the disciples through the ages from the narrowing of the broad scope of mission which, like every Christian task, must hinge on the motives of love and authenticity.'[41] The 'Great Commission' connected with the Great Commandment may be summarized as 'love in action.' This means that the mission of God should be applied to the entire person, the entire society, and the entire universe. Bosch clearly says, 'Mission is the church sent into the world, to love, to serve, to preach, to teach, to heal, and to liberate.'[42] Jesus,

---

[38] Bosch, *Transforming Mission*, 6.

[39] Bosch, *Transforming Mission*, 6.

[40] John R.W. Stott, *Christian Mission in the Modern World* (Downers Grove, IL: InterVarsity, 1975), 29-30.

[41] Hertig, 'The Jubilee Mission of Jesus in the Gospel of Luke', 149.

[42] Bosch, *Transforming Mission*, 412.

therefore, sent his disciples forth with a holistic 'down-to-earth' command.

Making a disciple is the ultimate goal of teaching. Discipleship entails time spent with people, working carefully with them, and bringing them to Christ in a gentle way. Discipleship means relationship to Christ, not just the simple given rules or principles of religion (Mt. 23:3). It is clear that leading people to yield and submit to the will of God is the purpose of discipleship. The holistic mission found in 'teaching them to obey everything I have commanded you' focuses on obedience to Christ following the period of discipleship.

IX. 'I Am with You' (Matthew 28:20)

Here is great and fresh assurance to Christ's disciples. In fact, this is more of a guarantee than a promise. Thus, it was not only a promise for the future. The verb denotes not a future, 'I will be with you'; the verb is the present tense and assured his disciples of an already existing reality. 'I am there with you.' 'You don't even have to think about this; I am already there.' 'I am with you' also means that 'I am your major resource', 'it is not even some divine attribute or provision.' It also reminds them not to trust in their own resources or human methods (Gal. 3:2-3). The ultimate supplier is 'I, myself.'[43]

Acts 2 reveals the spiritual presence of Jesus through the Holy Spirit. The promise was fulfilled at Pentecost. The Spirit of God who descended upon the disciples and gathered people at Pentecost continued to be with the church in the presence of Jesus Christ. They manifested Jesus' presence through their ministry in the Spirit and in power. The story of the seven sons of Sceva is a good example: the evil spirit said, 'Jesus I know, and I know about Paul, but who are you?' (Acts 19:15). The evil spirit recognized Paul because Jesus Christ was with him in the Holy Spirit. In Acts 28, Paul was protected from the bite of the viper. This could not have happened unless a supernatural power kept him, in other words, the presence of Christ was with Paul. John wrote of Jesus and the provision of the Holy Spirit in mission in much more detail (Jn. 14–17).

God's universal mission requires the promise of God's presence for fulfilment. Emmanuel (God with us) first appears in Isaiah 7:14 during a period of hopelessness when the hearts of the people were tormented by a cruel enemy assault. The 'God-with-us then was utilized in the context of an enemy threat (cf. Is. 8:8; Ex. 3:14).'[44] God's presence in the Old Testament declared, 'I will fight for you.'[45] Likewise, the mission of the

---

[43] Bruner, *Matthew*, II, 1105.

[44] Hertig, 'The Jubilee Mission of Jesus in the Gospel of Luke', 149.

[45] Bruner, *Matthew*, II, 1106.

disciples needed the presence of the resurrected Christ. Any attempt at mission without the presence of Jesus is sure to fail, as 'expressed in the sleep of the disciples at Gethsemane, their flight, betrayal by Judas and denial by Peter.'[46]

Jesus' promise to be with them 'always', to the very end of the age, denotes that his 'presence and mission' extend to 'the end of human history.' Thus, the 'Great Commission' is an 'eschatological mandate' to be fulfilled during the church period (cf. Mt. 24:14).[47] The Gospel of Matthew is ongoing. We enter the story at the 'Great Commission' text and join in his mission assignment as we near the end of the age (Mt. 24:14).[48] Jesus spent his life training and making disciples. This is expected to continue through the lives of his disciples.

X. Conclusion

Fulfilling the 'Great Commission' should be the primary work of the church. The 'Great Commission' exists for that purpose. This awareness needs to move the church into the harvest field to win souls. One would say that for effective mission (besides making disciples, baptizing, and proclaiming the Word) to succeed, employing dynamic methods matching the context is necessary. This is necessary. However, the mission of Jesus exemplifies the significance of relying on the Spirit in our mission. The messianic mission also demonstrates concern for all levels of people: the poor, the sick, the oppressed, and those both spiritually and physically blind. The 'Great Commission' reflects the passion and love of Jesus for the entire world.

In implementing the 'Great Commission' the guidance and leadership of the Holy Spirit must be the priority before considering human strategies and plans. The voice of Jesus must be heard for an efficient work of God. The disciples' mission in Acts is a prime example portraying the absolute direction and partnership of the Spirit. The promise of Jesus with you means the presence of the Holy Spirit with us until the end of the age.

The going, making disciples and baptizing is not only done as a duty but must be accomplished in the love of God. Love has to be reflected as the essence of the 'Great Commission.' When the church fulfills its mandate based on God's love, the commission will be genuinely established.

---

[46] B. Rod Doyle, 'Matthew's Intention as Discovered by His Structure', *Revue Biblique* 95 (January 1988), 51.

[47] Hertig, 'The Jubilee Mission of Jesus in the Gospel of Luke', 150.

[48] Hertig, 'The Jubilee Mission of Jesus in the Gospel of Luke', 150.

CHAPTER 7

The Geographical Expansion of the Church in Acts

There was phenomenal growth in the early church after the outpouring of the Holy Spirit. Acts 2:40-41 records how Peter was bold in preaching the gospel of salvation and repentance. He warned people, 'Save yourselves from this corrupt generation.' People who heard his message experienced the infilling of the Holy Spirit and about 3,000 people were saved that day. Verse 47 notes, 'and the Lord added to their number daily those who were being saved.' This account attests to the active work of the Spirit resulting in the extraordinary growth of the body of Christ.

According to Bruce Metzger[1] the church geographically experienced expansion to six locations. The first was throughout Jerusalem (Acts 1:1–6:7), as Acts 6:7 says, 'the word of God spread. The number of disciples in Jerusalem increased rapidly, and a large number of priests became obedient to the faith' (6:7). Acts 1:8 says 'and you will be my witnesses in Jerusalem....' The second region was throughout Palestine (6:8–9:31). 'Then the church throughout Judea, Galilee and Samaria enjoyed a time of peace. It was strengthened: and encouraged by the Holy Spirit, it grew in numbers, living in the fear of the Lord' (9:1). The third geographical expansion was beyond the Jewish boundaries (9:32–12:24): so Acts 12.24 records, 'the word of God continued to increase and spread'. The fourth location that the apostles reached was throughout Cyprus and into Central Asia Minor (12:25–16:5). Acts 16:5 reports, 'So the churches were strengthened in the faith and grew daily in numbers.' The fifth place was western Asia Minor (16:6–19:20): 'In this way the word of the Lord spread widely and grew in power' (19:20). The sixth and last location was Rome. During his journey to Jerusalem, Paul was arrested, but finally arrived at his destination, Rome (19:21–28:31).

Luke is not only concerned with church growth but also the victory of the new and liberating faith as it 'breaks through barriers that are

---

[1] Bruce Metzger, *The New Testament: Its Background, Growth and Content* (Nashville, TN: Abingdon, 1965), 239.

religious, racial and national.'[2] Each expansion of growth is discussed regarding its situation, beginnings, and elements of growth.

I. Jerusalem (Acts 1:1–6:7)

1.1 Situation

During the time Jesus' stayed with his disciples, he instructed them not to leave Jerusalem but to wait for 'what the Father has promised' (Lk. 24:49). This implies an anticipation of being filled with the Spirit. Jesus described the Holy Spirit on the night before his crucifixion (Jn. 14:16, 26; 15:26). Jesus' final words instructed the disciples to stay in Jerusalem until they were clothed with power from above. Three years of preparation was not enough for them to be effective witnesses. They needed divine assistance, the empowerment of the Holy Spirit. Acts 1:8 clearly explains why they were to remain in the city. Verse 8 states, 'But you will receive power when the Holy Spirit comes on you, and you will be my witnesses in Jerusalem, and in all Judea and Samaria, and to the ends of the earth.' They needed to be empowered to be witnesses. 'Witness' is connected to the old verb to wit, which is 'to know.' Consequently, a witness is a person who can testify on the basis of knowledge (cf. Is. 43:10-12). One must come to know Christ to bear witness to him.[3] Everett Harrison discusses the places where they would soon witness to Jesus:

> The place where the witness was to be exercised is comprehended in four terms which represent more specific direction than that given in Luke 24:47, and which geographically involve moving out from a center to the circumference, as ripples from a pebble dropped into a pond. The same terms may be viewed according to the degree of spiritual preparation found in these places. In Jerusalem and Judea Judaism held sway, and it rested on the revealed religion of the Old Testament. Samaria enshrined a religion partly true and partly false, a confused mixture (Jn. 4:22). The remotest part of the earth speaks of the unenlightened condition of paganism and heathenism, with false notions of God corrupting the ideals and life of society.[4]

Each of these places held its unique challenges to the disciples. Jerusalem had the blood of the prophets on its hands (Mt. 23:37), and now their hands were stained with the blood of Jesus of Nazareth. Judea was the home of Judas Iscariot, the betrayer. Samaria, with its traditional animosity toward Jews, had restricted the rights of travelers (Lk. 9:51-56).

---

[2] Luther E. Copeland, 'Who Really Sent the First Missionaries?', *Evangelical Missions Quarterly* 11:4 (1975), 233-39.

[3] Everett. F. Harrison, *Interpreting Acts: The Expanding Church* (Grand Rapids, MI: Zondervan, 1986), 39-40.

[4] Harrison, *Acts*, 40.

The farthest region of the earth was the place of the Gentiles (Is. 49:6), 'whose spiritual and moral uncleanness drew from Jews the epithet dogs.'[5]

Having reassured his disciples with the promise of the Father, Jesus ascended to heaven while the sheep without a shepherd obeyed and waited for the promise. Their feelings were a mixture of loss and anticipation.

1.2 Beginnings

Acts 2:4 describes the spiritual atmosphere of the gathering: 'All of them were filled with the Holy Spirit....' The baptism of the Spirit predicted by John and pledged afresh by Jesus became a reality. F.F. Bruce comments, 'Being filled with the Spirit was an experience to be repeated on several occasions (cf. 4:8, 31), but the baptism in the Spirit which the believing community now experienced was an event which took place once for all.'[6] The baptism in the Spirit was manifested when those gathered spoke in tongues. Visitors from different places heard and acknowledged the tongues uttered by the people in their Spirit baptism. They were pilgrims, Jews, and proselytes who were representatives of many lands and of various native dialects. They heard the believers praying and praising God in their own dialects and languages. Jerusalemites were also surprised to hear the host of languages that were not Aramaic or Greek, but the languages of Egypt, Asia Minor and Italy.[7]

In the early church it was essential to have criteria to determine whether such utterances came from God or not, just as it had been needed in Old Testament times.[8] Paul stated, as a clear but unerring test, that the utterance must bear witness to Jesus: 'no one can say "Jesus is Lord" except by the Holy Spirit' (1 Cor. 12:3). John insisted on a more specific test: 'every spirit which confesses that Jesus Christ has come in the flesh is of God' (1 Jn. 4:2). On the day of Pentecost, the content of the ecstatic language was praises for 'the mighty deeds of God' (v. 11). And the scope of the expression in which they were declared suggests the coming of the Spirit, especially in preparation for the worldwide proclamation of the gospel.[9]

---

[5] Harrison, *Acts*, 40.

[6] Bruce, *The Book of the Acts*, 51.

[7] P. Loyd, *The Holy Spirit in the Acts* (London: SCM, 1952), 32.

[8] Cf. Deut. 18:22, 'If what a prophet proclaims in the name of the Lord does not take place or come true that is a message the Lord has not spoken.' See also Deut. 13:1-5.

[9] K. Lake, *The Earlier Epistles of Paul* (London: Rivingtons, 1914), 241-52.

1.3 Description of Growth

People in Jerusalem came to the Lord through signs, wonders and the preaching of the Word of God. Acts 3 reports the healing of a crippled man, lame from birth. He was brought to the temple every day and used to beg from the people passing by (v. 2). One day Peter and John were about to enter the temple, and the lame man asked for money. But Peter answered, 'Silver or gold I do not have, but what I have I give you. In the name of Jesus Christ of Nazareth, walk.' Then, 'taking him by the right hand, he helped him up, and instantly the man's feet and ankles became strong. He jumped to his feet and began to walk....' The two apostles healed him by the name and authority of Jesus Christ of Nazareth. He sprang up, stood, and walked for the first time in his life. The power through which Jesus had healed many sick during his public ministry was still powerfully available to his disciples.

In Capernaum, Jesus healed a paralyzed man by commanding that he rise and walk. Peter used similar words now. Jesus' words used in healing the paralytic were intended to serve as the public validation of his authority to pardon sins as well as to heal the sick (Mk. 2:10-11). Thus, his disciples not only healed the sick in the name of Jesus but also obtained from him divine power and heavenly authority to declare the gospel and the remission of sins.[10]

Then, Peter began to proclaim Jesus by declaring what the mission of Christ the Messiah meant to Israel if only they would respond to him in faith (Acts 3:11-26).[11] Peter continued to preach boldly the gospel of Jesus' resurrection in the midst of many trials. Following the sensational healing in the temple, Peter was filled with the Holy Spirit and courageously spoke to the rulers and elders of how the crippled man was healed. Only through the name of Jesus of Nazareth could this man stand and receive salvation. This news of a remarkable miracle spread throughout Jerusalem (v. 16). The incident threatened religious people in high positions, causing anxiety. They ordered Peter and John not to speak and share the gospel of Jesus (vv. 17-18). However, the determination of the two apostles to preach was never quenched by persecution. F.F. Bruce observes, 'the healing of the cripple and the preaching which followed it had the effect of adding a large number to the three thousand who believed on the day of Pentecost. The number of men alone, says Luke, now totaled some five thousand.'[12] The arrest of Peter and John by Jewish authorities and their overnight jailing even heightened their commitment to witness (Acts 4:1-4).

---

[10] Bruce, *The Book of the Acts*, 79.

[11] Harrison, *Acts*, 71.

[12] Bruce, *The Book of the Acts*, 90.

Other miracles wrought through the apostles are found in Acts 5:12-16. These demonstrations of God's power and love drew multitudes, both female and male, to Christ as believers. A remarkable incident is found in verses 15-16:

> As a result, people brought the sick into the streets and laid them on beds and mats so that at least Peter's shadow might fall on some of them as he passed by. Crowds gathered also from the towns around Jerusalem, bringing their sick and those tormented by evil spirits, and all of them were healed.

The work of the Holy Spirit dynamically permeated Jerusalem and soon would expand to other regions.

II. Palestine: Judea, Galilee and Samaria (Acts 6:8–9:31)

2.1 Beginnings

At this time, as the believers increased in number, there was a complaint from the Hellenists, Greek-speaking Jews born abroad but now living in Jerusalem and worshipping in several synagogues (6:9). They were offended with the Hebrews or Aramaic-speaking Christians due to the neglect of their widows. 'The number of Hellenistic widows was relatively large, for many pious Jews in the evening of their days settled in Jerusalem so as to be buried near the Holy City; the widows of such men had no relatives at hand to look after them and tended to become dependent on public charity.'[13] Every Friday the local poor were helped. In addition, other groups called the 'poor strangers' received daily food and drink. However, the Christians probably no longer practised this system but may have introduced a new system of 'poor-relief distinct from the Jewish.' In other words, they were not cared for by the Jewish community and, eventually, were estranged from the synagogue.[14]

The twelve decided to call together the entire community to elect seven men of good reputation, full of the Spirit and wisdom. The apostles wanted to delegate to the seven this important task of caring. Here, the apostles were not overworked nor did they neglect their responsibility in the matter addressed above. But their intention was to look for wise and recognized men within the community to resolve this increasingly serious problem.[15]

Acts 6:4 notes the priority of the apostles: to spend their time in prayer and in the ministry of teaching. Prayer was a tradition not only inherited

---

[13] Ernst Haenchen, *The Acts of the Apostles: A Commentary* (Philadelphia, PA: Westminster, 1971), 261.

[14] Haenchen, *The Acts of the Apostles*, 262.

[15] Haenchen, *The Acts of the Apostles*, 262.

from Judaism but also practiced for the prosperity of the entire community.[16]

The elected men, after being prayed for by the apostles, made such an enormous impact that the number of believers in Jerusalem was multiplied and countless priests were added to the faith (6:1-7). Soon the apostles and the seven men crossed the boundary of Jerusalem and headed toward Palestine. A revival in Palestine started when one of the seven men, Stephen, was martyred.

2.2 Description of Growth

Verse 8 describes Stephen's spirituality: 'Now Stephen, a man full of God's grace and power, did great wonders and miraculous signs among the people.' It was through the laying on of apostolic hands that 'the Seven evidently receive (or rather, Stephen and Philip evidently receive) what Luke regards as the distinctive mode of the Spirit's activity in the missionary enterprise—the Spirit of God which confirms the word of God with signs and wonders.'[17] The 'great wonders and miraculous signs', including healing no doubt brought Stephen into favor 'among the people' (5:12-13).[18]

Stephen not only performed miracles but also presented his unique message in the synagogue of Jerusalem. There were several synagogues in Jerusalem but one Hellenistic synagogue in particular 'preceding A.D. 70 is known from a Greek inscription set up by its founder Theodotus and discovered on Ophel in 1913/14.'[19] It has been thought that this was the only synagogue to which Luke refers here.[20] Verses 13-14 mark that Stephen's preaching caused sharp opposition and perhaps a full-blown argument. It is believed that the Messiahship of Jesus was probably the primary focus of debate.[21] William Manson affirms that 'Stephen grasped and asserted the more-than-Jewish-Messianic sense in which the office and significance of Jesus in religious history were to be understood.'[22] Thus, the nature of his debate would be the main charge against him (7:13-14). People in the synagogue could not accept his revolutionary argument. Those who heard him speak rushed on him and stoned him to

---

[16] Haenchen, *The Acts of the Apostles*, 263.

[17] G.W.H. Lampe, *The Seal of the Spirit* (London: Longmans, 1951), 74.

[18] Bruce, *The Book of the Acts*, 124.

[19] Gustav Adolf Deissmann, *Light from the Ancient East: The New Testament Illustrated by Recently Discovered Texts of the Graeco-Roman World* (New York: George H. Doran, 1927), 439-41.

[20] Bruce, *The Book of the Acts*, 125.

[21] Bruce, *The Book of the Acts*, 125.

[22] W. Manson, *The Epistle to the Hebrews: An Historical and Theological Consideration* (London: Hodder and Stoughton, 1951), 31-32.

death (7:57-58). This generated further persecution of the church at Jerusalem and 'all except the apostles were scattered throughout Judea and Samaria' (8:1). Thus, their persecution and dispersion introduced the fulfilment of the risen Lord's commission to his disciples.

Philip, who came to Samaria, established an outstanding ministry. Acts 8:4-8 depicts Philip's work in that region:

> Those who had been scattered preached the word wherever they went. Philip went down to a city in Samaria and proclaimed the Christ there. When the crowds heard Philip and saw the miraculous signs he did, they all paid close attention to what he said. With shrieks, evil spirits came out of many, and many paralytics and cripples were healed. So there was great joy in that city.

Works of exorcism and healing characterized Philip's ministry. It was so remarkable that great numbers believed his message. As in the ministry of Jesus, and his disciples, the works of divine power were obvious signs affirming the message that he declared.

In 8:10-11, Simon the sorcerer was known as a man who had obtained 'Great Power' (v. 10). Simon so thrilled his fellow men with his magic powers that people considered him a great man of the supreme God, the channel both of almighty power and of divine revelation.[23] However, Simon himself was awestruck by the proclamation of the Word and the power manifestations of Philip (8:11, 18). Perhaps this occasion was similar to the magicians of Egypt in the presence of Moses. They acknowledged that the messenger of the God of Truth possessed a source of power that outstripped their own. Simon and his followers came to a total turning point and were baptized. They stayed in Philip's company.

Philip's mission among the Samaritans prompted Peter and John to evangelize other Samaritan communities as they took the southward road to Jerusalem (v. 25).

III. Mission Outside Jewish Boundaries (Acts 9:32–12:24)

The third expansion was outside the Jewish boundaries. The apostles were beginning to reach the Gentile community.

3.1 Beginnings

A new horizon in the ministry of the disciples opened when they were pushed to make a decision regarding their attitude toward the Gentiles. The issue had already presented itself with the conversion of the Ethiopian eunuch; however, this did not have a lasting influence on the

---

[23] Bruce, *The Book of the Acts*, 167.

church. Once converts were conformed to church life their acceptability was not questioned.

First, Luke writes of how the matter arose for the Jerusalem Christians as an outcome of the conversion of Cornelius and his household. Second, he records how the church in Antioch became active in witnessing until the time more Jewish and Gentile believers were added. The basic decision to preach the gospel to the Gentiles was, therefore, made although the issue of whether the Gentiles should live the way the Jews lived continued to perplex the church.[24]

We cannot help but recognize the Holy Spirit's call to the Gentiles. Peter came to Joppa by an invitation from Cornelius and with an order from God (10:32). His presence was significant to Cornelius and his family as they received salvation and the baptism of the Holy Spirit. Peter acted as the agent of Jesus in performing mighty miracles similar to those of Jesus in the Gospels. This story is the first miracle account of Peter among the Gentiles beyond Jerusalem, Judea and Samaria.

3.2 Description of Growth

In Acts 10, the invitation of God to the Gentiles is recorded and the subsequent outpouring of the Holy Spirit. Cornelius was a God-fearing man who offered daily prayers and was known to help the needy. This man was a centurion, the backbone of the Roman army. When the battle was the fiercest, these soldiers were ready to give their own lives.[25] The starting point came from Cornelius' vision and his obedience (10:3-8). God's specific order through the vision was to go to Joppa, thirty miles south, and fetch Peter. This incident powerfully illustrates that salvation was offered to all humanity, using human agency (Lk. 24:47).

Peter's vision of unclean animals in his prayer time held the crucial revelation of opening the gospel to the Gentiles. It was also to accomplish God's purpose of establishing a close relationship between the Jew and Gentile. Peter reacted strongly against God's command to 'kill and eat' unclean animals. However, the divine voice came a second time saying that all God's creatures are clean and not harmful. This entire transaction took place three times. God revealed his will to bring salvation to the Gentiles.

Having been invited by Cornelius, Peter presented the message of peace through Jesus Christ, the universal provision of salvation, and the Lordship of Christ (10:35-36). The blessing of salvation was received by those Gentiles who heard, believed and responded quickly to the Word

---

[24] I. Howard Marshall, *Acts*, Tyndale New Testament Commentaries (Grand Rapids, MI: Eerdmans, 1986), 177.

[25] Larkin, *Acts*, 155.

from Peter (10:44-48). Subsequently the Spirit fell on them as Peter preached the message.

The salvation of the Gentiles was divinely planned and fulfilled. It was complete and genuine. God proved that the gathering Gentiles had indeed been granted 'repentance unto life' (11:18) by pouring out the Spirit on them as he had done on Jewish believers at Pentecost (2:4, 17, 33).[26] 'Its authenticity was manifested by the Gentiles' speaking in tongues.'[27]

Geographical growth continued. Acts 11:19-24 depicts the scattering of believers resulting from the martyrdom of Stephen. It was seized as an opportunity to evangelize a different ethnic group, the Jews of Phoenicia. They had moved to Cyprus in earlier times and by the first century AD a large Jewish territory had been established. Hellenistic Jewish Christians from Cyprus and Cyrene went immediately to witness to Jesus to the Gentiles while maintaining evangelism to the Jews (10:20).[28]

Barnabas was a crucial figure and served as a bridge to the Gentiles at Antioch. He was described as 'a good man, full of the Holy Spirit and faith' and contributed in bringing 'a great number to the Lord' (11:24). Barnabas then recruited Paul as his companion in the gospel. For an entire year they worked together in the church and were involved in teaching many people.[29] It is noted that teaching and evangelism were not exclusive ministries and, although each was distinct, they were undivided. Larkin clearly affirms that

> In a day when a misapplication of church growth theory's 'homogeneous unit principle' can produce monocultural churches, God's blessing on inclusive evangelism across ethnic lines at Antioch is a necessary reminder of where God's heart is. While he may indeed give growth within homogeneous ethnic units, such units are not his ideal, and neither should they be ours.[30]

IV. Mission to Cyprus and Central Asia Minor (Acts 12:25–16:5)

4.1 Beginnings

Paul's method was to stay in one location until he had established the stability of a community of believers, or until he was pushed to leave by circumstances outside his control. The same fundamental principles were

---

[26] Max M.B. Turner, 'Spirit Endowment in Luke/Acts: Some Linguistic Considerations', in Max M.B. Turner (ed), *Biblical and Historical Essays from London Bible College* (London: London Bible College, 1981), 12: 45-63.

[27] Larkin, *Acts*, 168.

[28] Larkin, *Acts*, 175.

[29] Harrison, *Interpreting Acts*, 196.

[30] Larkin, *Acts*, 177.

actually followed on his 'missionary campaign' in Asia Minor (cf. 13:50; 14:3, 5-7, 20).[31]

The following story is significant in that it describes the first 'overseas mission' program fulfilled by people of a chosen church, rather than by single individuals. It was started under the inspiration of the Spirit, rather than as a result of persecution.[32] In Acts 13:1-3 Barnabas and Paul ministered at Antioch and were joined by three others. All five had the gifts of prophecy and teaching. They began to assume a central place in the life of the church and ministered with Spirit-endowed gifts. The Spirit who appoints leaders in the church spoke through prophetic utterance that the church should send two outstanding leaders, Paul and Barnabas, to God-designated places. Thus, God himself instituted mission. Finally, the church commissioned Paul and Barnabas by the laying on of hands. It was an act of blessing wherein the church allied itself with them and committed them to the grace of God (14:26).

4.2 Description of Growth

Actually, there had been some evangelism in Cyprus (11:19) before Paul and Barnabas reached this region. It was not far from Antioch, only sixty miles away from the seaport of Seleucia. Paul's interactions with the Roman governor and his conflict with a magician who went against Paul's preaching of the Word of God were the primary moves of evangelism. Paul definitely was a gifted evangelist.

The Spirit led Paul into a confrontation with the forces of evil (11:9). Paul collided with a Jew who practiced magic and declared himself to be a prophet. He was perhaps the same type as Sceva, who claimed to be a Jewish high priest in Ephesus (19:14). This sorcerer had two names, 'Bar-Jesus', and 'Elymas.' It was common for Jews to have more than one name and the latter meant 'magician'.[33] This sorcerer (13:8) opposed the ministry of Paul and Barnabas to the proconsul. Paul, full of the Spirit, confronted him. Acts 13:9-11 records Paul's exercise of spiritual authority in his encounter with the sorcerer.

> Then Saul, who was also called Paul, filled with the Holy Spirit, looked straight at Elymas and said, 'You are a child of the devil and an enemy of everything that is right! You are full of all kinds of deceit and trickery. Will you never stop perverting the right ways of the Lord? Now the hand of the Lord is against you. You are going to be blind, and for a time you will be unable to see the light of the sun.'

---

[31] Marshall, *Acts*, 214

[32] E. Best, 'Acts 13:1-3', *Journal of Theological Studies* 11 (1960), 344-48.

[33] Marshall, *Acts,* 219.

The unfortunate sorcerer was afflicted with a mistiness of the eyes and became blind as Paul had decreed. The divine power linked with the teaching of the missionaries certainly amazed the proconsul to such an extent that he became a Christian. Here again Luke stresses that teaching and the power encounter, two parallel sources, are important to manifest the living God and are a means of drawing people to Him.

After ministry in Cyprus, Paul and his companion headed to Antioch in Pisidia where they sought a contact point for the Word of God in the synagogue. Paul's preaching began with the Jews and proselytes or God-fearing Gentiles. His message was substantial and lengthy. It could be summarized as a historical study designed to root the coming of Jesus in the kingly succession of Judah and to show that the work of Jesus was a fulfilment of prophecy. It culminated in an invocation to the listeners not to repeat the foolishness of the people of Jerusalem who had deserted Jesus. Paul continued his historical sermon pointing to the significance of Jesus' resurrection and interpreting it in the light of the Scriptures.[34]

The Gentiles who heard Paul's message received it whole-heartedly, rejoiced at the good news, and praised the Word of God. The latter phrase went along with 2 Thessalonians 3:1, implying that the Lord is glorified when people receive his Word and believe it.[35] The ministry of Paul's preaching led the Gentiles to the Lord.

Acts 14:8-20 tells of a miracle at Lystra and people coming to Christ through that incident. A man was healed (vv. 8-10) who heard the message and had faith. The missionaries were regarded as gods in human form and the bystanders who heard of the miracle wanted to pay them honor. This misunderstanding compelled Paul to speak to the people about the true God. Apparently, the healing miracle made a way for the gathering people to know the almighty and powerful God.

Chapter 14:21-23 addresses successful evangelism in Derbe. Paul and Barnabas not only visited churches along the way, they also preached the gospel, made many disciples (v. 21), and continued to move from one place to another for evangelism. Verse 28 reports how God marvelously opened doors to reach the Gentiles and made them his disciples.

V. Western Asia Minor (Acts 16:6–19:20)

5.1 Beginnings

Paul certainly used strategy in planning and was very sensitive to the guidance of the Spirit of God. After visiting the churches established in South Galatia with Barnabas, Paul and his companions continued their mission journey along the westward road to Ephesus (16:6). However, the

---

[34] Marshall, *Acts*, 221.
[35] Marshall, *Acts*, 230-31.

Holy Spirit prevented them from taking this road. The prohibition was apparently given before they went through the Phrygian and Galatian region, 'probably the Phrygian territory incorporated in the province of Galatia, in which Iconium and Pisidian Antioch lay.'[36]

The Spirit changed their plans. Evidently going into the Asian regions was not the will of God. They began to go in the direction of Bithynia in northwest Asia Minor with its Greek cities, but the Spirit forbade them to go there a second time. Thus, instead of continuing north into Bithynia they turned west to the sea at Troas.[37]

At Troas, Paul had a night vision. A Macedonian man stood imploring Paul to cross over to Macedonia and assist the people there. 'Macedonia, which became the dominant power in the Greek world and western Asia under Philip II and Alexander the Great in the fourth century B.C., had been a Roman province since 146 B.C.'[38] Because of the vision, Paul was assured that the Spirit was leading them to Macedonia.

5.2 Description of Growth

Philippi was the first Macedonian church that Paul and his companions visited. Around 42 BC 'the town became a Roman colony, i.e., a settlement for veteran Roman soldiers who possessed the rights of self-government under Roman law and freedom from taxes.'[39] The first recipients of the gospel in that place were women who associated with the 'Jewish faith.'[40] Among the women gathering for prayer was a lady called Lydia who traveled from Thyatira, a town in Asia Minor. Lydia was also, in fact, the name of the place where adherents of the Jewish religion lived.[41] A merchant in purple cloth, Lydia listened to the message of Paul that may have related the coming of the Messiah in the human form of Jesus (cf. 17:3). Lydia's conversion led her household to baptism. The typical household was large; a system of extended family, including slaves. Green states that 'Roman households were united in a common religious cult irrespective of age or personal beliefs.'[42] The conversion of this woman, head of her household, either alone or a widow, had important spiritual implications for the members of the household. Hulbert's application for evangelism in the present time from this text is

---

[36] Bruce, *The Book of the Acts*, 306.

[37] Bruce, The Book of the Acts, 306.

[38] Bruce, *The Book of the Acts*, 307.

[39] R.P. Martin, *Philippians*, New Century Bible Commenatry (London: Oliphants, 1976), 2-9.

[40] Marshall, *Acts*, 266.

[41] Marshall, *Acts*, 267.

[42] Michael Green, *Evangelism in the Early Church* (Grand Rapids, MI: Eerdmans, 1970), 210

well taken. He relates that believers today should be concerned about creating 'social networks' for the rapid spread of the word of God. Through this strategy, one can expect multi-household conversions, which may snowball into 'people movements' (16:6–19:20).[43]

From Philippi Paul headed on his journey towards the capital city of Macedonia, Thessalonica, where he was fruitful in the Jewish synagogue. Paul and his company won many converts among the Jews, the Gentile adherents and the women (17:1-9). They were known as leading women, which might imply that they were members of the upper class in the town; alternatively, it means 'wives of the leading men.' It was clearer in some early textual witnesses.[44]

Paul's effective evangelism among the Gentiles stirred up the envy of the Jews. They searched for Paul and Silas in Jason's house to accuse them. However, at night they were taken to Berea. The Berean Jews and God-fearers were of 'noble character' with openness and willingness to be taught.[45] Verse 11 reads, 'for they received the message with great eagerness and examined the Scriptures.' As a result, many Jews and Greeks, outstanding women as well as men, perhaps both God-fearers and pagans, believed the message and were saved (17:12).

After Berea, Paul went to Athens, which was full of idols. Paul's evangelism consisted of reasoning 'about Jesus and the resurrection' (17:18). He debated day by day with those who happened to be nearby. Verse 22 records Paul's speech to the Areopagus. The gospel was preached to pagans, 'even cultured pagans like the members of the Court of the Areopagus' with a declaration of the living and true God. Then he concluded his message (17:31) by saying that God, who was the Creator of all, was also God the judge of all. God had already established a day he would 'judge the world in righteousness.'[46] Paul's preaching to the Athenians was not very fruitful but the seed of the gospel planted in that city would bear fruit in due time.

Acts 19 describes Paul's ministry and miracles in Ephesus. According to verse 13 there were people who wandered about 'making a living by various kinds of pseudo-scientific or clairvoyant powers, including the practice of exorcism.'[47] They invoked the names of any god or spirit. Frequently they invoked long lists of names to be sure of involving the proper god in any occasion. Even pagans utilized the diverse Jewish

---

[43] Terry C. Hulbert, 'Families are Both the Means and Goal of Evangelism', *Evangelical Mission Quarterly* 14 (1978), 171-77.

[44] Marshall, *Acts*, 278.

[45] Johannes P. Louw and Eugene A. Nida, *Greek-English Lexicon of the New Testament Based on Semantic Domains* (New York: United Bible Societies, 1988), 332.

[46] Bruce, *The Book of the Acts*, 340.

[47] Marshall, *Acts*, 311.

names of God. Jewish exorcists, the seven sons of Sceva (cf. Lk. 11:9), tried to use the name of Jesus to compete with Paul's power.[48]

One day, an evil spirit challenged these Jewish exorcists by saying, "'Jesus I know, and I know about Paul, but who are you?" Then the man who had the evil spirit jumped on them and over-powered them all' (19:15-16). This man beat them to the point of bleeding and they ran naked out of their house. When the news spread among the Jewish and Geek communities, people were seized with fear. Thus, the name of Jesus was lifted up in high honor. Verses 19-20 explain that this incident had a great effect on various people, including religious practitioners:

> A number who had practiced sorcery brought their scrolls together and burned them publicly. When they calculated the value of the scrolls, the total came to fifty thousand drachmas. In this way the word of the Lord spread widely and grew in power.

VI. Rome (Acts 19:21–28:31)

6.1 Beginnings

The Spirit guided Paul to conclude his ministry of church planting in Ephesus. He had already planned other missions. He wanted to revisit Macedonia and Achaia before going back to Jerusalem. One of Paul's ministries was to encourage young churches (14:22-23; 15:36, 41; 18:23). His final destination was Rome (23:11; Rom. 1:13-15; 15:30-32) and he was adamant that he must see Rome, not for personal enjoyment but to preach the gospel (19:21).

Paul continued to pursue his call to the Gentiles. He strongly believed that he was chosen to win the souls of the Gentiles. His conversion was intended to reach to the ends of the earth, 'even the regions of the west, including Spain', which he also desired to evangelize through his own personal efforts (9:15; 26:22; Rom. 15:24).[49]

Paul had a definite mission strategy under the Spirit's guidance. As a strategic thinker and an efficient planner, Paul was able to work effectively. Churches today need to be strategic under the leadership of the Spirit.

6.2 Paul's Final Mission Journey

Paul continued his ministry of preaching the Word. In Ephesus, he was caught in a riot which erupted in connection with a silver smith named

---

[48] Hans Dieter Betz, *The Greek Magical Papyri in Translation, including the Demotic Spells* (Chicago, IL: University of Chicago Press, 1986), 96.

[49] Larkin, *Acts*, 280.

Demetrius, who made silver shrines of Artemis which brought in a great deal of business for the craftsmen (19:24). His primary complaint was that Paul converted large numbers of people in Ephesus, and practically the entire area of Asia (19:26). Demetrius was also afraid that his business would receive a bad name and he might lose his income. There were some other concerns from this man (19:26-27). Due to severe rioting Paul could not stay there any longer but had to depart. Persecution, in a sense, caused Paul and his companions to be stronger and bolder and to proceed with their mission.

The sermon at Miletus concluded Paul's missionary work. From there he went to Jerusalem where he was arrested and imprisoned, went through diverse trials, and eventually was taken to Rome to appear before the Emperor.

Similarities can be seen in the ministries of Jesus and Paul. Jesus, too, went to Jerusalem, and spoke prophetically concerning his forthcoming sufferings; he was charged and tried, and appeared before the Jews and the Romans. He further foretold that his suffering would lead to his death and resurrection. Marshall notes that 'Paul literally experienced death and resurrection in Acts, but some have seen in his last journey, with his salvation from possible death by shipwreck and drowning, a pattern similar to the experience of Jesus' (cf. 2 Cor. 1:8-10).[50]

VII. Conclusion

Jesus commanded his disciples to spread the good news before he ascended into heaven and they went out to an unseen mission field. As the Holy Spirit empowered them with the Word and power, they tirelessly ministered to the people, moving from one place to another. This dynamic mission drew large numbers of people, both Jews and Gentiles, to the Kingdom of God.

Paul's conversion and unbending commitment to the Gentiles were crucial in the geographical expansion of the church. The message of salvation crossed the Jewish boundaries to the Gentiles who received it more favorably. Paul no longer felt responsibility solely to the Jews. Paul gladly said, 'this is my gospel for which I am suffering even to the point of being chained like a criminal. But God's word is not chained' (2 Tim. 2:8-9). Paul expressed a sense of ownership and stewardship toward the gospel. This strong commitment to the gospel should continue in the church today.

---

[50] Marshall, *Acts*, 337.

CHAPTER 8

Incarnational Mission

The Son of God entered this world of pain and suffering and modeled incarnational mission. Born into a particular culture, he took on a human body and willingly associated with people different from himself. The Supreme Being fit in with no intention of removing the existing culture. He adapted.

This is an important model for missionaries who serve in a foreign country. One of the ways to identify with the local people is to be incarnated into the receptor's culture. John Stott affirms, 'The incarnation was the most spectacular instance of cultural identification in the history of humankind.'[1] How will we as missionaries become incarnated?

I. Love

Jesus emptied himself of heavenly glory and lowered himself to servitude. He was born in human form, lived a human life, experienced human agony and sorrows, took the sins of humanity upon himself and died the death of a human being. Jesus identified intimately with humanity. He did it because he loves mankind. It is a model for all involved in mission. It is clear that genuine mission is incarnational mission, demonstrating the love of God. What exactly is the biblical love that we are to display? There are several references concerning love in the Bible. Among them, 1 Corinthians 13 is the primary description of the kind of love Christians should exhibit in their lives and on the mission field.

The entire chapter of 1 Corinthians 13 portrays love pictorially and dynamically reveals the uniqueness of the believers' way of life. 1 Corinthians 13:4-7 notes the attributes of love:

> Love is patient, love is kind. It does not envy, it does not boast, it is not proud. It
> is not easily angered, it keeps no record of wrongs. Love does not delight in evil

---

[1] John R.W. Stott, 'Our Challenge for Today: Keynote Address of the European Leadership Conference on World Evangelization' (European Leadership Conference on World Evangelization, September 5-9, 1988 in Stuttgart, Germany).

but rejoices with the truth. It always protects, always trusts, always hopes, always perseveres.

The verb employed in the first sentence, 'love is patient', is the opposite of 'short-tempered.' It means having patience with people rather than circumstances. Thus, patience refers to the character of a God-like person.[2] Patience is required for every work in God's Kingdom. To identify with the people we work with we must grow in patience. If one is impatient it is difficult to stay in one place long enough to acquire the necessary language and knowledge of another's ways. Jesus demonstrated his eminent patience with diverse groups of people even to the moment of crucifixion.

The next description of love is kindness. Love shows goodness towards those who have dealt one harm; it gives itself in kindness, in service to others. This is also a primary attitude of Kingdom workers when cultivating a relationship with people. Building relationships in God-reflecting kindness and goodness is a key to incarnational mission.

Next, one who loves is not envious. Paul's confession that he became a Greek to the Greeks, a Jew to the Jews, poor to the poor and rich to the rich implies his identification with the different circumstances of people. Such identification only comes when one does not compare oneself to others. Comparison with people often brings unnecessary envy. Paul's disarming stance teaches us to embrace all people in society, whether of high or low position without comparison and jealousy.

Because love is not rude, one is expected not to behave in disreputable and dishonorable ways. Furthermore, authentic love is not self-centered. This love keeps no record of wrongs. Love does not remember past mistakes or hold a grudge. Love does not subtract from another's merits or keep records of faults. It listens to no stories of evil. Love never harbors a sense of injury.[3]

The love taught in 1 Corinthians is a foundation for incarnational mission. This is what Jesus Christ demonstrated in his ministry, and Paul did in his mission work. Thus, this should be the model of our mission.

II. Knowing People's Thought World

Cross-cultural workers are called to merge into other people's spheres of thought; the world of their thinking and ideas. James Sire defines the meaning of 'naturalism', 'nihilism', 'existentialism', and 'deism' in his

---

[2] Leon Morris, *The First Epistle of Paul to the Corinthians* (Grand Rapids, MI: Eerdmans, 1989), 736.

[3] Morris, *The First Epistle of Paul to the Corinthians*, 736.

book, *The Universe Next Door: A Basic Catalogue of World Views.*[4] Stott rephrases the definition in his own words:

> He refers to each of these ideologies or world views as a universe next door, another universe, an alien universe of thought to our own Christian world view, and it will take an incarnation to enter into that other universe, to seek people for Christ.[5]

Bishop Lesslie Newbigin, who has been a missionary, discusses his perspective of entering another's thought world. He questions the relationship between the western believer's worldview in light of what the Gospels teach. Newbigin grieves over the manner in which Christians retreat from the public forum into their own privatized secure arena. He wrestles with himself, not wanting to approach hurting people with theology from a narrow western perspective. It is time for Christians to 'challenge the scientific worldview that is central to western culture and its reductionist claim to be able to explain everything.' It is also the time for believers to 'challenge the atheistic materialism that is at the foundation both of capitalism and communism.' The church should assert that the foundational structures of a nation's life should not remain empty. If Christ is not present, an idol will surely occupy its space.[6]

It is believed that we have to call forth the current generation of Christian thinkers, who will serve with their God-given minds, to challenge other cultures with the declarations of Jesus Christ. They must be thinkers who will take the initiative to expose profane culture, to reveal its emptiness, and bring the gospel of Jesus Christ to lost people. Thus, Jesus can be understood to offer men and women what other ideologies cannot give them; he alone can fulfill all human desires and dreams. We as Christian workers need to learn to get into 'other people's thought worlds.'[7]

Entering people's thinking patterns is crucial not only to understand them but also to present the gospel incarnationally through their cultural structures and thoughts. The entire Bible is an articulation of witness to God's relationship with humans and communicating with them on their own cultural levels. God converses with his creatures, Adam and Eve, in the Garden. He talks with different characters such as Abraham, Moses, David, and others within altering Hebrew cultural environments. And he became the living Word who lived in time and space as a person in Jewish society. Peter's preaching and Paul's message to the Areopagus in

---

[4] James W. Sire, *The Universe Next Door: A Basic Worldviews Catalog* (Downers Grove, IL: Inter-Varsity, 1976), 48-49, 61-62, 76-77, 101-102.

[5] Stott, 'Our Challenge for Today', 34.

[6] Lesslie Newbigin, *Foolishness to the Greeks: The Gospel and Western Culture* (Grand Rapids, MI: Eerdmans, 1986), 53-57.

[7] Stott, 'Our Challenge for Today', 34.

Athens reveal how they were prepared to meet their listeners. The Gospels and Epistles also address congregations in diverse cultures in different ways. This teaches that all genuine communication of the gospel in mission must be patterned from within a community's own culture.[8]

How does the gospel connect to human cultures? The gospel is God's self-revelation in history through his deeds, and supernaturally through his incarnation. The relationship of God's revelation in the Scriptures to human cultures complements and can be understood by the analogy to Christ's incarnation. Just as Christ was absolutely God, but became fully human without diminishing his deity, so also the gospel is God's revelation, but is communicated by way of human cultures without losing its divine character.[9]

Incarnating the gospel is to present the message in another's thought world and realm, while maintaining the authenticity and value of the Christian message. If the good news is compromised by the people and deviated from in its appropriateness, the gospel cannot offer what it should be offering.

III. Understanding People's Heart Worlds

Cross-cultural workers need to learn to enter into others' heart worlds; their wounds, hurts and the realm of their alienation and agony. Sharing comforting messages is necessary, but touching hearts in concrete service is also as important as the message. In other words, this indicates a place for social concern in relation to evangelism, or at least, this is one of motivations for it. Stott presents this issue well.

> Just as it was not possible for missionaries in Africa to ignore the evils of polygamy or slavery, just as it is not possible for missionaries in Asia, or particularly India, not to oppose caste, the dowry system, child marriage and sarti, just as it is not possible for missionaries in Latin America to turn a blind eye to the exploitation of Indian tribes, or the great and appallingly degrading poverty of the masses, so it is not possible in Europe to disregard the plight of the deprived, the immigrant, the homeless, the unemployed and the alienated youth.[10]

Missionaries have to enter into people's hearts because enthusiastic care for their needs is one component of the incarnation. Stott further states that the Christian faith may only be proven when faith is enacted. This happens by going out and entering into 'the doubts of the doubters, the

---

[8] Paul Hiebert, *Anthropological Insights for Christian Witness* (Grand Rapids, MI: Baker, 1985), 54-55.

[9] Hiebert, *Anthropological Insights*, 53.

[10] Stott, 'Our Challenge for Today', 34.

questions of the questioner or the loneliness of those who have lost the way.'[11]

Countless lonely people need a touch from those who know how to comfort with the genuine love of Christ. Paul accurately addresses what it means to be a person who will identify with crying and agonizing people. Romans 12:15-16 exhorts, 'Rejoice with those who rejoice, mourn with those who mourn. Live in harmony with one another. Do not be proud but be willing to associate with people of low position. Do not be conceited.' Unfortunately, Christians are hesitant to identify with people in these various conditions, particularly those who are mourning. We tend to separate ourselves from them, as if they are living in another world.

Philip Yancey's book, *What's So Amazing about Grace?*, reports the response of Christians with cold hearts to the neglected. Yancey confesses his experience with a gay person who had a bitter experience with Christians.[12]

> I started making it a point to meet other gay people in our neighborhood, including some who came from a Christian background. 'I still believe', one told me. 'I would love to go to church, but whenever I've tried someone spreads a rumor about me and suddenly everyone withdraws.' He added a chilling remark, 'As a gay man, I've found it's easier for me to get sex on the streets than to get a hug in church.[13]

We also need to explore other areas of the world, those from which Christians tend to keep their distance. Jesus' life is a prime example in terms of associating with all types of people. Jesus did not let an institution interfere with his love for each individual. Jewish ethnic and religious policies did not allow him to engage in conversation with a Samaritan woman. 'This woman, rejected by Jews on account of her race, rejected by neighbors on account of her serial marriages, became the first missionary appointed by Jesus.' His disciples included a tax collector, seen as a traitor by Israel, and also a 'Zealot', a member of the 'superpatriot party.' Jesus acknowledged the 'countercultural' John the Baptist. He met with Nicodemus, an observant Pharisee, and with a Roman centurion. He ate in the home of another Pharisee named Simon and in the home of an 'unclean' man, Simon the Leper. For Jesus, 'the person was more important than any category or label.'[14]

For the good news to be holistic, the gospel bearers need to know how to use differing methods. Furthermore, they should seek to understand the hearts of the poor, the rich, the broken, and the weeping. It is

---

[11] Stott, 'Our Challenge for Today', 34.

[12] Philip Yancey, *What's So Amazing about Grace?* (Grand Rapids, MI: Zondervan, 1997), 168.

[13] Yancey, *What's So Amazing about Grace?*, 152.

[14] Yancey, *What's So Amazing about Grace?*, 152.

necessary to comprehend the value and role of the gospel and to have a Christ-like heart. In this way one will not only reach out and touch the surface of people's lives but also touch them at their deepest level.

IV. Suffering

Biblical mission models in this postmodern century should not separate the suffering and death of Jesus. The mission of Jesus was completed and perfected only through his death, a full sacrifice. Mission without paying the cost of taking up the cross is only partial fulfilment of the mission. Whether it is emotional, mental, physical, or environmental suffering, we have to take up the cross. Are we willing to pay the cost for being an incarnational missionary? Are we willing to go to the neglected places where there may be no running water or functioning sanitary system? Will we travel an unpaved road shaped and misshapen by rocks that even the trucks and sturdy vehicles struggle to get across? In this postmodern generation, a missionary's understanding of biblical concepts may not include suffering. They may regard this element of mission as relegated to the days of old, something our forefathers needed to do but something which is certainly not necessary today. The example that Jesus lived was not only applicable in a certain age but applies to each believer until the end of time, until Jesus returns.

The Messiah, the suffering Servant, is seen clearly in the book of Isaiah. Chapter 53 depicts his intense suffering to save people's souls. It is a serious matter. Rescuing lost souls from darkness anticipates a conflict between the two spiritual realms: the powers of darkness and God's power. The Scriptures record that Jesus gave his back to those who beat him, his cheeks to those who slapped and spit upon him. He was scorned and deserted by men, familiar with suffering and given over to death. The Servant must encounter hardship, whereby the mission is effective. John Stott says it well: 'Every form of mission leads to some form of the cross. The very shape of mission is cruciform and we can understand mission only in terms of the cross.'[15]

Jesus demonstrated and lived biblical principles and he extended them to his followers. His life was so simple he did not even have a place to sleep and to eat (Lk. 9:58). Yet, he was content. It seems that earthly contentment was not his primary focus. Jesus sought only to fulfill the mission given him by his Father. When the Greeks visited Jesus he spoke of something meaningful: unless a kernel of wheat falls into the ground and dies, it remains alone, but if it dies, it multiplies (Jn. 12:24). Death is

---

[15] Stott, 'Our Challenge for Today', 34.

the 'condition of fruitfulness. For the One who died it meant the salvation of souls.'[16]

Paul applies the principle to himself. Ephesians 3:13 says, 'that you should not be discouraged because of my sufferings for you which are your glory.' 2 Timothy 2:10: 'I endure everything for the sake of the elect in order that they may obtain salvation with eternal glory.' 2 Corinthians 4:12: 'So then, death is at work in us, but life is at work in you.' I believe that these three Scriptures of Paul are among the most significant messages in the entire New Testament. Paul boldly claims that through his suffering others will walk into glory, that through his perseverance, others will come into a circle of blessing, and that through his death, others will receive eternal life. It is not, of course, that he refers to any 'atoning efficacy to his sufferings and death, as he does to the sufferings and death of Jesus.'[17] People may obtain salvation, life and glory only when the gospel is shared by those who deliver the good news of God faithfully, without hesitation or fear of suffering.

As the Pauline message clearly states, Paul was imprisoned because of the gospel he proclaimed. He was also imprisoned due to Jewish resistance to the gospel of salvation for the non-Jewish. Are we willing to suffer for God and his mandate? We believers tend to be triumphalistic and inclined to a prosperity gospel. We sometimes easily overlook the tribulation and hardship that is unavoidable for the sake of the gospel. The incarnation in our mission takes place when we join in his suffering. 'Are we ready to die with Christ to popularity and promotion, to comfort and success, to our arrogant sense of personal or cultural superiority, or to our selfish ambition to be famous or rich or powerful?'[18] It is the seed which dies that will multiply in God's mission.

V. The Holy Spirit: The Gift for Mission

John addresses a central issue: the 'Spirit bearer' is also the 'Spirit giver.' He is the One who 'baptizes with' the Spirit and 'sends' the Spirit to his disciples (Jn. 1:42; 15:26; 16:7). He notes the commission of Jesus to his disciples, '"As the Father has sent me, I am sending you." And with that he breathed on them and said, "Receive the Holy Spirit"' (20:21-22). However, the gift of the Spirit is not able to be given until he is glorified, which means 'ascended, exalted, enthroned.'[19]

Jesus was sent by the Spirit. When he was baptized in water, the Spirit came upon him and led him into the desert. The Holy Spirit is the One who made his earthly life and mission incarnational. Messianic mission in

---

[16] Stott, 'Our Challenge for Today', 34.

[17] Stott, 'Our Challenge for Today', 34.

[18] Stott, 'Our Challenge for Today', 35.

[19] J.I. Packer, *Keep in Step with the Spirit* (Grand Rapids, MI: Baker, 1997), 87.

Luke 4 indicates clearly the significant role of the Spirit. Only after being empowered was the Messiah able to launch his mission among the poor, the sick, and the outcast to meet their heartfelt needs. His compassion and love could only be actually incarnated through the power of the Spirit. The disciples received the Spirit not merely to fulfill the Great Commission, preach the gospel and make people disciples of Christ, but also to accomplish incarnational mission. Stott states very clearly:

> The true fact is that only the Spirit of God can take the Word spoken in human weakness and carry it home with power in the mind, the heart, the conscience, the will of the hearers. Only the Holy Spirit opens the eyes of the blind to see the truth as it is in Jesus. Only the Holy Spirit unstops the ears of the deaf to listen to the voice of Christ and opens the mouths of the dumb to confess that he is Lord.[20]

Sociological strategy and communications skills are important in evangelism and bringing people into God's Kingdom. However, we need to beware that they do not decrease our reliance and trust in the work and the power of the Holy Spirit. Furthermore, they may hinder us as we seek to obtain the heart for incarnational mission we must have if we are to identify with the people. Only the Spirit can bring us into this realm and heart.

VI. Conclusion

Incarnational mission is what Jesus demonstrated. His true identification came when he genuinely associated with people on their own level. He was willing to bend his supremacy. This humility draws people into God's Kingdom. This lifestyle of humility is an excellent model that we as workers and followers of Jesus need to adopt. Paul's attitude toward the gospel is identical to that of Jesus.

What kind of mission are we attempting to accomplish? Are we forging ahead using only human methods while leaving the biblical principles of mission behind? Incarnational mission requires sacrifice, humility, flexibility, and love. If we omit these elements, we are not suitably engaged in God's mission. Twenty-first century mission may need elements of contextualization but we have to remember that a mission of incarnation is the foundation for all mission.

---

[20] Stott, 'Our Challenge for Today', 36.

'Children, Our Children'

Children are important in God's Kingdom. Jesus loves children and he tells his disciples to become like them. Sadly, children are often neglected and overlooked. In many cases, they feel hopeless. For children of the mountain tribes in northern Luzon this is the case. Thankfully, one area of considerable benefit is education. Several years ago, we started focusing on children and their future by sending them to school.

Darwin Cayso is a six-year old boy, born and raised in Bagu, located deep in the mountains. He lost his father when he was still an infant. So Darwin grew up and was raised by his single, widowed mother. He is unusually short for his age, much like his parents, but he is fortunate, growing up as the only child receiving the full attention and love from his family. This is quite unusual as most families have an average of twelve children, receiving little care from their parents.

Schooling as a Divine Blessing

Darwin is very blessed because of his opportunity to attend an elementary school, just a few miles away from his home. Going to school everyday is not easy during the rainy season which lasts six to seven months. Rains are strong and very damaging to homes and property. After eating breakfast, the village children eagerly head to school passing through sweet potato and rice fields. Even though they are barefoot and the bottoms of their feet are harder than Nike shoes, they run much faster than those with good rubber shoes. They are content with something as insignificant as an empty gasoline container to entertain them while running to school.

For Christian parents, to be able to send their children to school is not only a privilege but also a blessing from God. Schools are rarely seen, and can be found in few villages. Children from a nearby village called Igig-ang also attend this school. There are only fifteen families in this village and the children have to walk much farther than those from Bagu. Going to school is not easy: over a hanging bridge with a river underneath, hiking through a thick forest up a steep, narrow trail. This is a road not made for young children and women, but for vigorous men. Many people have to climb across sturdy branches to go across the trail.

Children in Strong Rain

I remember climbing down this road during a heavy downpour of rain. Most of the way I slid on my bottom. Needless to say, it was impossible to walk on such a slippery road. The heavy rain frequently causes landslides, causing inconvenience to the villagers. The village children during these times cannot reach their school house, it is virtually impossible even to start. Often parents wait until their children become strong enough to hike across mountain trails for several hours during rainy days. Thus, many start their education at the age of nine or ten. It is a real blessing if one survives to the age of ten. Because of poor living conditions and no medical service, children easily become sick and die. In fact, only half of a family's children are expected to survive.

On my second visit to Igig-ang, it was not easy to descend from 5,000 feet to 2,500 feet. It was a sunny, hot day and I was extremely thirsty and very exhausted from the hike. Knowing I was thirsty, young children quickly climbed up a coconut tree. They effortlessly climbed to the top and picked a young coconut, containing fresh juice, thus quenching my thirst and refreshing me. I felt their hospitality and love, inevitably urging me to come back again.

Are Children for Work or Study?

Often children help their parents in the fields. This is in addition to studying, housework, and looking after younger siblings, and creates an understandable burden. When the children are absent from the village, usually at school, the place is very quiet, with only a couple of pigs, chickens, and dogs keeping the houses company. Villagers live in traditional homes known as nipa huts. A thatched roof covers the one room hut and it is adjoined to a tiny kitchen. The straw ceilings inside become black from the smoke from the cooking fires.

Suddenly, a child cries out in intense pain breaking the silence of the village; a startled pig squeals. A man nearby coughs sharply from tuberculosis, constantly spitting saliva.

I entered one home, and after adjusting my eyes to the dark, I found a baby wrapped in a blanket on the floor. The baby was suffering from physical sickness but there was no means for healing; the only way is to call to the spirits through the help of a village priest.

Can the Spirits Heal?

These tribal people are sensitive to the spiritual world. It is believed that the spirits of the dead can return to the vicinity of the village or family to help with the problems of immediate family members. This notion has been inherited from the ancestors, and is passed down from generation to generation. Thus, when a family member is sick, help is sought from the spirits. However, animal sacrifices are necessary to communicate with the spirit world. As the leader of the village, the village priest gives all prescriptions and procedures as to how the sacrifice should be conducted. Rituals vary according to the specific problem. The more rituals that need to be offered the greater the number of sacrifices that are needed. Purchasing pigs is extremely costly for those who do not have a steady income. Frequently, people are forced to borrow money from relatives or neighbors, increasing their debts.

Villagers, who do not have access to medical services, have no choice but to expect miracles from the spirits after sacrificing animals. Like this family, often the parents simply leave their suffering baby on the floor in darkness to go to work in the field. Unless the baby has a strong immune system, which most young children in the villages lack, it is extremely unlikely the infant will survive. The parents endure unimaginable anguish as they plant their sweet potatoes, the source of their small income. Obviously, all of the villagers in these regions, but especially the mountain children, are underprivileged and unfortunate.

Suffering Children

Most houses in the mountains have chickens and roosters. Is the life of her ailing child comparable with that of a chicken? Definitely not! Didn't the mother have a hard time during her nine months of pregnancy? At dusk, she hurries home to check on the condition of her baby. She hopes that the baby will be crying as loud as it had been that morning. She knows that if the cry is weak, the baby is likewise weak. As a mother, I can imagine that her heart's cry to the gods of her ancestors is an expression of her desperation.

This incident is very simple and is almost insignificant when compared with the tragedies of some of the other children. At one point, all of the children in the village were suffering from vomiting, diarrhea and high fever because of an epidemic that took many lives. Drinking water from a river is often unsafe and causes many to become ill. Most villages do not have a water system, although there is such a great need for one. Often missionaries bring such knowledge and help. In addition, most of the children are suffering from malnutrition; their skinny bodies cannot sustain the ravages of disease, causing the children to appear as withered leaves. Though the mother may have twelve other children, losing the life of one is surely painful. Her heart is full of agony, grief, and questions, which she will carry as a burden throughout her entire life. Many memories will remind her of her lost son. As she comes back from the fields and hears her children playing together, or while feeding them, she will remember her dead son. She must be suffering emotional torment, which will be lifelong.

Is It too Difficult to Finish the Elementary School?

It is understood among these people that sending a child to elementary school is somehow more important than sending one to college. It is an occasion of great celebration for a child to be admitted to elementary school.

There were three young girls in Igig-ang who were able to attend school at the age of ten. They studied well and reached the fifth grade. However, one of them decided to marry in her teen years, which is quite common. Soon her tummy showed. It was funny in the eyes of her two friends who accompanied her to school. They talked to each other, saying, 'Shall we get married and give up school?' Young mothers bear many children, continuing to bear sometimes until the age of fifty. Hence, it seems that finishing elementary school is not easy at all. You can imagine the joy and happiness of parents and children alike on graduation day.

Darwin in Bagu eventually graduated from elementary school at the age of sixteen. He did not want to marry early and have many children, as did all his friends. Darwin was determined to pursue his education. Since there is no high school in the village, he decided to work to raise the money for him to go to high school in Baguio City. After announcing his desire to his family, he left home. For four years he worked very hard, but never earned enough because most of it went on housing and living expenses. Time went by quickly and Darwin turned twenty.

After many years of hard work, Darwin's dream came true. He was accepted into high school in Tuding, a city in Itogon, near Baguio. He squeezed in to sleep with the children of a missionary in a small room. As he studied for four years in high school, the missionary's care and support for Darwin affected him in a marvelous way. He proudly graduated from high school. Darwin was among the first to graduate from his high school. Soon after, many more children from Bagu, his hometown, were sent to high school.

The Kalangoya tribe is unique with about twelve children attending a school in a Kankana-ey village. It is very far away and difficult to get to. The children are eager to study, and on the other side of the world in Southern California, some women working in a factory have 'adopted' the children of this tribe. Their children also joined in this adoption project. Twelve women and their families each contribute ten dollars a month to support the children's education. It not only covers tuition fees but also the expenses for dormitory, uniforms, and many other things. The mountain children's parents are very happy because their children can go to school. However, it makes their work harder because their children are unable to help them in the rice fields during the day.

One summer, when I visited a group of these mountain children who were just finishing their afternoon meal, we held hands to show unity with the families in Southern California. Part of the messages that came from them was, 'We have not forgotten you. We support you. We pray for you. We save the last pennies in our pockets for you. We wish you great success in the future.' One Christmas, each of the children received a Bible, a colorful Christmas card, and some pictures as gifts enclosed in a brown envelope from California. It is something that these growing young men and women for Christ will never forget.

Bibliography

Ackroyd, P.R., *The Second Book of Samuel*, The Cambridge Bible Commentary (Cambridge: Cambridge University Press, 1977)

Albertz, Rainer, 'Die "Antrittspredigt" Jesu im Lukasevangelium auf ihrem alttestamentlichen Hintergrund', *Zeitschrift für die Neutestamentliche Wissenschaft und die Kunde der Alteren Kirche* 74:3-4 (1983), 182-206

Allen, Roland, *The Ministry of the Spirit: Selected Writings by Roland Allen*, ed. David M. Paton (Grand Rapids, MI: Eerdmans, 1962)

Alter, Robert, *Genesis: Translation and Commentary* (London and New York: Norton, 1996)

Alsup, John E., 'Typology', *The Anchor Bible Dictionary*. Vol. 6. ed. David N. Freedman (New York: Doubleday, 1992)

Anderson, A.A., *2 Samuel*, Word Biblical Commentary 11 (Dallas TX: Word, 1989)

Barclay, William, *The Gospel of Luke*, Daily Study Bible (Philadelphia, PA: Westminster, 1975)

Beker, Christian, *Paul and Apostle: The Triumph of God in Life and Thought* (Philadelphia, PA: Fortress, 1982)

_____, *Suffering and Hope: The Biblical Vision and the Human Predicament* (Philadelphia, PA: Fortress, 1987)

Bergquist, James A., 'Good News to the Poor: Why Does This Lucan Motif Appear to Run Dry in the Book of Acts?', *Bangalore Theological Forum* 28:1 (1987), 18-27

Best, E., 'Acts 13:1-3', *Journal of Theological Studies* 11 (1960), 344-48

Betz, Hans Dieter, *The Greek Magical Papyri in Translation, Including the Demotic Spells* (Chicago, IL: University of Chicago Press, 1986)

Block, Daniel I., *Judges, Ruth*, New American Commentary (Nashville, TN: Broadman & Holman, 1999)

Blomberg, Craig L., *Matthew*, New American Commentary: An Exegetical and Theological Exposition of Holy Scripture (Nashville, TN: Broadman, 1992)

Bosch, David J., *Transforming Mission: Paradigm Shifts in Theology of Mission* (Maryknoll, NY: Orbis, 1993)

Brown, Robert M., and Elie Wiesel, *Messenger to All Humanity* (Notre Dame, IN: University of Notre Dame Press, 1983)

Bruce, F.F., *Acts*, New International Commentary on the New Testament (Grand Rapids, MI: Eerdmans, 1988)

Brueggemann, Walter, *First and Second Samuel*, Interpretation: A Bible Commentary for Teaching and Preaching (Louisville, KY: John Knox, 1973)

Bruner, Frederick Dale, 'Matthew', *Dialogue* 34 (1995), 312-20

Budd, Philip J., *Numbers*, Word Biblical Commentary 5 (Waco TX: Word, 1984)

Butler, Trent C., *Joshua*, Word Biblical Commentary (Waco, TX: Word, 1983)

Carson, D.A., *The Gospel according to John* (Grand Rapid, MI: Eerdmans, 1991)

Cassuto, U., *A Commentary on the Book of Exodus* (Jerusalem: Magnes, 1987)

_____, *A Commentary on the Book of Genesis 1-11*, trans. I. Abrahams (Jerusalem: Magnes, 1964)

_____, *Exodus* (Jerusalem: Magnes, 1987)

Cole, Robert Alan, *Exodus: An Introduction and Commentary* (Downers Grove, IL: Inter-Varsity, 1973)

Copeland, Luther E., 'Who Really Sent the First Missionaries?', *Evangelical Missions Quarterly* 11:4 (1975), 233-39

Craddock, Fred B., *Luke* (Louisville, KY: Westminster/John Knox, 1990)

Danne, James, *The Freedom of God* (Grand Rapids, MI: Eerdmans, 1973)

Deissmann, Adolf, 'Light from the Ancient East', *Concordia Journal* 5:2 (1979), 439-41

DeVries, S.J., *Prophet against Prophet* (Waco, TX: Word, 1985)

Dillon, Richard J., 'Easter Revelation and Mission Program in Luke 24:46-48', in D. Durken (ed), *Sin, Salvation and the Spirit* (Collegeville: Liturgical, 1979), 253-265

Douglas, J.D. (ed.), *New Bible Dictionary*, 2nd edn (Leicester: Inter-Varsity Press, 1982)

Doyle, B. Rod, 'Matthew's Intention as Discovered by His Structure', *Revue Biblique* 95 (1988), 51-54

Dupont, Jacques, *The Salvation of the Gentiles: Essays on the Acts of the Apostles* (New York: Paulist, 1979)

Durham, John I., *Exodus*, Word Biblical Commentary 3 (Waco, TX: Word, 1987)

Earle, Ralph, *Mark* (Grand Rapid, MI: Zondervan, 1957)

Ellis, Peter F., *Matthew: His Mind and His Message* (Collegeville, MN: Liturgical Press, 1974)

Endo, Shusaku, *Silence*, trans. W. Johnston (London: Peter Owen, 1976)

Fewell, Danna and David Gunn, *Compromising Redemption: Relating Characters in the Book of Ruth* (Louisville, KY: John Knox Press, 1990)

France, R.T., *Matthew: Evangelist and Teacher* (Grand Rapids, MI: Zondervan, 1989)

Gardner, Richard B., *Matthew* (Grand Rapids, MI: Eerdmans, 1991)

Gaventa, B.R., 'You Will Be my Witness: Aspects of Mission in the Acts of the Apostles', *Missiology* 10 (1982), 413-25

Geldenhuys, Norval, *The Gospel of Luke*, The New International Commentary on the New Testament (Grand Rapids, MI: Eerdmans, 1979)

Glasser, Arthur F., *Kingdom and Mission* (Pasadena CA: Fuller Theological Seminary, School of World Mission, 1989)

Gray, John, *1 and 2 Kings* (London: SCM, 1970)

Green, Michael, *Evangelism in the Early Church* (Grand Rapids, MI: Eerdmans, 1970)

Guelich, Robert, *The Sermon on the Mount* (Waco, TX: Word Books, 1982)

Gundry, Robert H., *Matthew: A Commentary on His Literary and Theological Art* (Grand Rapids, MI: Eerdmans, 1982)

Haenchen, Ernst, *The Acts of the Apostles: A Commentary* (Philadelphia, PA: Westminster, 1971)

_____, 'The Acts of the Apostles', *Scottish Journal of Theology* 25 (1972), 475-76

Hahn, Ferdinand, *Mission in the New Testament*, trans. Frank Clarke (London: SCM Press, 1965)

Hare, D.R.A. and D.J. Harrington, '"Make Disciples of All the Gentiles' (Mt. 28:19)', *Catholic Biblical Quarterly* 37 (1975), 359-69.

Harris, R. Laird, Gleason L. Archer, Jr., and Bruce K. Waltke (eds.), *Theological Wordbook of the Old Testament*, vol. 1 (Chicago, IL: Moody, 1980)

Harrison, Everett. F., *Interpreting Acts: The Expanding Church* (Grand Rapids, MI: Zondervan, 1986)

Hedlund, Roger E., *Mission to Man in the Bible* (Madras: Evangelical Literature Service, 1985)

Hendriksen, William, *Exposition of the Gospel according to Luke*, New Testament Commentary (Grand Rapids, MI: Baker, 1978)

Hertig, Paul, 'The Great Commission Revisited: The Role of God's Reign in Disciple Making', *Missiology* 29:3 (2001), 343-53

_____, 'The Jubilee Mission of Jesus in the Gospel of Luke' (unpublished paper, 1997)

Hertzberg, Hans Wilhelm, *1 and 2 Samuel: A Commentary*, trans. J.S. Bowden (Philadelphia, PA: Westminster, 1964)

Hiebert, Paul, *Anthropological Insights for Christian Witness* (Grand Rapids, MI: Baker, 1985)

Hobbs, T.R., *2 Kings*, Word Biblical Commentary 13 (Waco, TX: Word, 1985)

Hubbard, Benjamin Jerome, *The Matthean Redaction of a Primitive Apostolic Commissioning* (Missoula, MT: Scholar's Press, 1974)

Hulbert, Terry C., 'Families are Both the Means and Goal of Evangelism', *Evangelical Mission Quarterly* 14 (1978), 171-17

Ironside, Allen H., *Gospel of Luke* (Neptune, NJ: Loizeauz Brothers, 1968)

Jamieson, Robert, *Genesis-Deuteronomy* (Grand Rapids, MI: Eerdmans, 1945)

Joachim, Jeremias, *Jesus' Promise to the Nations* (London: SCM, 1966)

Kaiser, Walter C. Jr, 'Israel's Missionary Call', in Ralph D. Winter and Steven C. Hawthorne (eds.), *Perspectives on the World Christian Movement* (Pasadena, CA: William Carey Library, 1992)

_____, *Mission in the Old Testament* (Grand Rapids, MI: Baker, 2000)

Keil, C.F. and F. Kelitzsch, *The Pentateuch*, Commentary on the Old Testament 1, trans. James Martin (Grand Rapids MI: Eerdmans, 1981)

Kenyon, Dame K., *The Bible and Recent Archaeology* (Atlanta, GA: John Knox, 1978)

Kight, George A., *Isaiah 40-66: Servant Theology*, International Theological Commentary (Edinburgh/Grand Rapids, MI: Handsel/Eerdmans, 1984)

Kio, Stephen F. Hre, 'Understanding and Translating "Nation" in Matthew 28:19', *Bible Translator* 41 (1990), 230-38

Kittel, Gerhard and Gerhard Friedrich, *Dictionary of the New Testament*, Abridged in one volume by Geoffrey W. Bromiley (Grand Rapids, MI: Eerdmans, 1985)

Kraybill, Donald B., *The Upsidedown Kingdom* (Scottdale, PA: Herald Press, 1990)

Lake, K., *The Earlier Epistles of Paul* (London: Rivingtons, 1914)

Lambdin, Thomas O., *Introduction to Biblical Hebrew* (New York: Scribners, 1971)

Lampe, G.W.H., *The Seal of the Spirit* (London: Longmans, 1951)

Larkin, William J. Jr, *Acts*, IVP New Testament Commentary (Downers Grove, IL: Inter-Varsity Press, 1995)

LaVerdiere, Eugene A. and William G. Thompson, 'New Testament Communities in Transition', *Theological Studies* 37:4 (1976), 567-97

Leupold, H.C., *Exposition of Genesis*, vol. 1 (Grand Rapid, MI: Baker, 1984)

Lincoln, C. Eric, *Race, Religion and the Continuing American Dilemma* (New York: Hill and Wang, 1984)

Louw, Johannes P. and Eugene A. Nida, *Greek-English Lexicon of the New Testament Based on Semantic Domains*, vol. 2 (New York: United Bible Societies, 1988)

Loyd, P., *The Holy Spirit in the Acts* (London: SCM, 1952)

Ma, Julie C., *When the Spirit Meets the Spirits* (Frankfurt am Main: Peter Lang, 2000)

_____, 'Manifestation of Supernatural Power in Luke-Acts and the Kankana-ey Tribe of the Philippines', *Spirit and Church* 4:2 (2002), 109-28

Maarsingh, B., *Numbers: A Practical ComAmentary*, trans. John Vriend (Grand Rapids, MI: Eerdmans, 1985)

Manson, Williams, 'The Epistle to the Hebrews: An Historical and Theological Reconsideration', *Journal of Theological Studies* 5 (1954), 96-98

Marshall, Howard, *Acts*, Tyndale New Testament Commentary (Grand Rapids, MI: Eerdmans, 1986)

Martin, Ralph P., *Philippians*, New Century Bible Commentary (London: Oliphants, 1976)

Mays, Jame L., *Ezekiel, Second Isaiah*, Proclamation Commentaries (Philadelphia, PA: Fortress, 1978)

Mazamisa, L.W., *Beatific Comradeship: An Exegetical-Hermeneutical Study on Lk 10:25-37* (Kampen: Kok, 1987)

McKenzie, John L., *Second Isaiah*, Anchor Bible (Garden City, NY: Doubleday, 1968)

_____, 'The Elders in the Old Testament', *Biblica* 40:2 (1959), 522-40

Meier, John P., *A Marginal Jew: Rethinking the Historical Jesus*, vol. 1 (New York: Doubleday, 1994)

Metzger, Bruce, *The New Testament: Its Background, Growth and Content* (Nashville, TN: Abingdon, 1965)

Meyer, F.B., *Devotional Commentary on Exodus* (Grand Rapids, MI: Kregel, 1978)

Morris, Leon, *The First Epistle of Paul to the Corinthian* (Grand Rapids, MI: Eerdmans, 1989)

_____, *The Gospel according to Matthew* (Grand Rapids, MI: Eerdmans, 1992)

Murphy, Roland E., *Genesis*, Jerome Biblical Commentary (Englewood Cliffs, NJ: Prentice-Hall, 1968)

Newbigin, Lesslie, *Foolishness to the Greeks: The Gospel and Western Culture* (Grand Rapids, MI: Eerdmans, 1986)

Nielsen, Kirsten, *Ruth* (Louisville, KY: Westminster/John Knox, 1997)

Nineham, D.E., *The Gospel of St. Mark* (New York: Seabury, 1968)

Noth, Martin, *Numbers: A Commentary* (Philadelphia, PA: Westminster, 1968)

Packer, J.I., *Keep in Step with the Spirit* (Grand Rapids, MI: Baker, 1997)

Ratschow, C.H., 'Ist Gott angesichts der Leiden in der Welt zu rechtfertigen?' in C.H. Ratschow (ed.), *Von den Wandlungen Gottes* (Berlin: Walter de Gruyter, 1986)

Sanders, Jack T., 'The Parable of the Pounds and Lucan Anti-Semitism', *Theological Studies* 42 (1981), 660-68.

Schottroff, L. and W. Stegemann, *Jesus and the Hope of the Poor*, trans. Matthew J. O'Connell 1986 (Maryknoll, NY: Orbis, 1986)

Scott, Waldron, *Karl Batth's Theology of Mission* (Downers Grove, IL: Inter-Varsity Press, 1978)

Scullion, John, *Isaiah 40-66*, Old Testament Message 12 (Wilmington, DL: Michael Glazier, 1982)

Senior, Donald P., 'The Foundations for Mission in the New Testament', in Donald P. Senior and Carroll Stuhlmueller (eds.), *The Biblical Foundations for Mission* (Maryknoll, NY: Orbis Books, 1983)

Shank, David A., 'Jesus the Messiah: Messianic Foundation of Mission', in Wilbert R. Shenk (ed.), *The Transfiguration of Mission: Biblical, Theological, and Historical Foundations* (Scottdale, PA: Herald, 1993)

Shenk, Wilbert R., 'The Relevance of a Messianic Missiology for Mission Today', in Wilbert R. Shenk (ed.), *The Transfiguration of Mission: Biblical, Theological, and Historical Foundations* (Scottdale, PA: Herald, 1993)

Sire, James W., *The Universe Next Door: A Basic World Views Catalog* (Downers Grove, IL: Inter-Varsity Press, 1976)

Skinner, John, *Genesis: Critical and Exegetical Commentary* (Edinburgh: T. & T. Clark, 1969)

Soggin, Alberto, *Joshua: A Commentary* (Philadelphia, PA: Westminster, 1972)

Stein, Robert H., *Luke*, New American Commentary: An Exegetical and Theological Exposition of Holy Scripture 24 (Nashville, TN: Broadman Press, 1992)

Stott, John R.W., *Christian Mission in the Modern World* (Downers Grove, IL: Inter-Varsity Press, 1975)

_____, 'Our Challenge for Today: Keynote Address of the European Leadership Conference on World Evangelization' (European Leadership Conference on World Evangelization, Sept. 5-9, 1988, Stuttgart, Germany)

Sundker, Bengt, *The World of Mission* (Grand Rapids, MI: Eerdmans, 1965)

Tippet, Alan, *People Movements in Southern Polynesia* (Chicago, IL: Moody, 1971)

Towner, W. Sibley, '"Blessed Be YHWH" and "Blessed Art Thou, YHWH": The Modulation of a Biblical Formula', *Catholic Biblical Quarterly* 30 (1968), 386-99

Triebel, Johannes, 'Leiden als Thema der Missionstheologie', *Jahrbuch Mission* 20 (1988), 8-15

Trilling, Wolfgang, *Das wahre Israel: Studien zur Theologie des Matthaus-Evangeliums* (Munich: Kosel-Verlag, 1964)

Turner, Max M.B., 'Spirit Endowment in Luke/Acts: Some Linguistic Considerations', in Max M.B. Turner (ed.), *Biblical and Historical Essays from London Bible College* (London: London Bible College, 1981), 12, 45-63

Verseput, Donald J., 'The Davidic Messiah and Matthew's Jewish Christianity', *Society of Biblical Literature Seminar Papers* 34 (1995), 102-16

Wellhausen, J., *Die Composition des Hexateuchs und der historischen Bücher des Alten Testaments* (Berlin: W. de Gruyter, 1963)

Wenham, Gordon J., *Genesis 1-15*, Word Biblical Commentary 1 (Waco, TX: Word, 1987)

_____, *Numbers: An Introduction and Commentary* (Downers Grove, IL: Inter-Varsity Press, 1981)

Westermann, Claus, *Genesis 1-11: A Commentary*, trans. John J. Scullion (Minneapolis, MN: Augsburg, 1984)

_____, *Genesis: A Practical Commentary*, trans. David E. Green (Grand Rapids, MI: Eerdmans, 1985)

_____, *Isaiah 40-66*, Old Testament Library, trans. David M.G. Stalker (Philadelphia, PA: Westminster, 1969)

Whybray, R.N., *The Second Isaiah*, Old Testament Guides (Sheffield: JSOT Press, 1983)

Wilson, Stephen G., *The Gentiles and the Gentile Mission in Luke-Acts* (Cambridge: Cambridge University Press, 1973)

Wolff, H.W., 'Das Kerygma des Jahwisten', *Evangelische Theologie* 24:2 (1964), 73-98

Yancy, Philip, *What's So Amazing about Grace* (Grand Rapids, MI: Zondervan, 1997)

Youngblood, Ronald F., *Exodus*, Everyman's Bible Commentary (Chicago, IL: Moody Press, 1983)

Zingg, Paul, 'Die Stellung des Lukas zur Heidenmission', *Neue Zeitschrift für Missionswissenschaft* 29 (1973), 200-209

Author Index

Scripture Index

New Testament

Regnum Studies in Mission

Academic Monographs on Missiological Themes

(All titles paperback, 229 x 152mm)

Allan Anderson and Edmond Tang (eds.)
Asian and Pentecostal
The Charismatic Face of Christianity in Asia
(Published jointly with Asia Pacific Theological Seminary)
This book provides a thematic discussion and pioneering case studies on the history and development of Pentecostal and Charismatic churches in the countries of South Asia, South East Asia and East Asia.
2005 / 1-870345-43-6 / approx. 350pp

Ivor Mark Beaumont
Christology in Dialogue with Muslims
A Critical Analysis of Christian Presentations of Christ for Muslims from the Ninth and Twentieth Centuries
This book analyses Christian presentations of Christ for Muslims in the most creative periods of Christian-Muslim dialogue, the first half of the ninth century and the second half of the twentieth century. In these two periods, Christians made serious attempts to present their faith in Christ in terms that take into account Muslim perceptions of him, with a view to bridging the gap between Muslim and Christian convictions.
2005 / 1-870345-46-0 / xxvi + 228pp

Kwame Bediako
Theology and Identity
The Impact of Culture upon Christian Thought in the Second Century and in Modern Africa
The author examines the question of Christian identity in the context of the Graeco–Roman culture of the early Roman Empire. He then addresses the modern African predicament of quests for identity and integration.
1992 / 1-870345-10-X / xviii + 508pp

Gene Early
Leadership Expectations
How Executive Expectations are Created and Used in a Non-Profit Setting
The author creates an Expectation Enactment Analysis to study the role of the Chancellor of the University of the Nations-Kona, Hawaii, and is grounded in the field of managerial work, jobs, and behaviour, drawing on symbolic interactionism, role theory, role identity theory, and enactment theory. The result is a conceptual framework for further developing an understanding of managerial roles.
2005 / 1-870345-30-4 / approx 300pp

Keith E. Eitel
Paradigm Wars
The Southern Baptist International Mission Board
Faces the Third Millennium

The International Mission Board of the Southern Baptist Convention is the largest denominational mission agency in North America. This volume chronicles the historic and contemporary forces that led to the IMB's recent extensive reorganization, providing the most comprehensive case study to date of a historic mission agency restructuring to continue its mission purpose into the 21st century more effectively.

1999 / 1-870345-12-6 / x + 140pp

Tharcisse Gatwa
The Churches and Ethnic Ideology in the Rwandan Crises 1900-1994

Since the early years of the twentieth century Christianity has become a new factor in Rwandan society. This book investigates the role Christian churches played in the formulation and development of the racial ideology that culminated in the 1994 genocide.

2005 / 1-870345-24-X / approx 340pp

Bishop Gideon Githiga
The Church as the Bulwark against Authoritarianism
Development of Church and State Relations in Kenya,
with Particular Reference to the Years after
Political Independence 1963-1992

'All who care for love, peace and unity in Kenyan society will want to read this careful history by Bishop Githiga of how Kenyan Christians, drawing on the Bible, have sought to share the love of God, bring his peace and build up the unity of the nation, often in the face of great difficulties and opposition.'
Canon Dr Chris Sugden, Oxford Centre for Mission Studies.

2002 / 1-870345-38-X / xviii + 218pp

Samuel Jayakumar
Dalit Consciousness and Christian Conversion
Historical Resources for a Contemporary Debate
(Published jointly with ISPCK)

The main focus of this historical study is social change and transformation among the Dalit Christian communities in India. Historiography tests the evidence in the light of the conclusions of the modern Dalit liberation theologians.

1999 / 81-7214-497-0 / xxiv + 434pp

Samuel Jayakumar
Mission Reader
Historical Models for Wholistic Mission in the Indian Context
(Published jointly with ISPCK)
This book is written from an evangelical point of view revalidating and reaffirming the Christian commitment to wholistic mission. According to Jayakumar, the roots of the 'wholistic mission' combining 'evangelism and social concerns' are to be located in the history and tradition of Christian evangelism in the past; and the civilizing purpose of evangelism is compatible with modernity as an instrument in nation building.
2003 / 1-870345-42-8 / x + 250pp

Myung Sung-Hoon and Hong Young-Gi (eds.)
Charis and Charisma
David Yonggi Cho and the Growth of Yoido Full Gospel Church
This book discusses the factors responsible for the growth of the world's largest church. It expounds the role of the Holy Spirit, the leadership, prayer, preaching, cell groups and creativity in promoting church growth. It focuses on God's grace (charis) and inspiring leadership (charisma) as the two essential factors and the books purpose is to present a model for church growth worldwide.
2003 / 1-870345-45-2 / xxii + 218pp

Bernhard Ott
Beyond Fragmentation: Integrating Mission and Theological Education
A Critical Assessment of some Recent Developments in Evangelical Theological Education
Beyond Fragmentation is an enquiry into the development of Mission Studies in evangelical theological education in Germany and German-speaking Switzerland between 1960 and 1995. This is carried out by a detailed examination of the paradigm shifts which have taken place in recent years in both the theology of mission and the understanding of theological education.
2001 / 1-870345-14-2 / xxviii + 382pp

Bob Robinson
Christians Meeting Hindus
An Analysis and Theological Critique of the Hindu-Christian Encounter in India
This book focuses on the Hindu-Christian encounter, especially the intentional meeting called dialogue, mainly during the last four decades of the twentieth century, and mainly in India itself.
2004 / 1-870345-39-8 / xviii + 392pp

Christopher Sugden
Seeking the Asian Face of Jesus
*The Practice and Theology of Christian Social Witness
in Indonesia and India 1974–1996*
This study focuses on contemporary wholistic mission with the poor in India
and Indonesia combined with the call to transformation of all life in Christ
with micro-credit enterprise schemes. 'The literature on contextual theology
now has a new standard to rise to' – Lamin Sanneh (Yale University, USA).
1997 / 1-870345-26-6 / xx + 496pp

Christopher Sugden
Gospel, Culture and Transformation
*A Reprint, with a New Introduction, of Part Two of
Seeking the Asian Face of Jesus*
Gospel, Culture and Transformation explores the practice of mission
especially in relation to transforming cultures and communities. Vinay
Samuel has played a leading role in developing the understanding of mission
as transformation, which he defines as follows: 'Transformation is to enable
God's vision of society to be actualised in all relationships: social, economic
and spiritual, so that God's will may be reflected in human society and his
love experienced by all communities, especially the poor.'
2000 / 1-870345-32-0 / viii + 152pp

Hwa Yung
Mangoes or Bananas?
The Quest for an Authentic Asian Christian Theology
Asian Christian thought remains largely captive to Greek dualism and
enlightenment rationalism because of the overwhelming dominance of
Western culture. Authentic contextual Christian theologies will emerge
within Asian Christianity with a dual recovery of confidence in culture and
the gospel.
1997 / 1-870345-25-8 / xii + 274pp

regnum

Regnum Books International
9 Holdom Avenue
Bletchley
Milton Keynes MK1 1QR
United Kingdom

Web: www.authenticmedia.co.uk/paternoster

December 2004